UNDERSTANDING MICHAEL CHABON

UNDERSTANDING CONTEMPORARY AMERICAN LITERATURE

Matthew J. Bruccoli, Founding Editor

Linda Wagner-Martin, Series Editor

Volumes on

Edward Albee | Sherman Alexie | Nelson Algren | Paul Auster
Nicholson Baker | John Barth | Donald Barthelme | The Beats
Thomas Berger | The Black Mountain Poets | Robert Bly | T. C. Boyle
Raymond Carver | Michael Chabon | Fred Chappell | Chicano Literature
Contemporary American Drama | Contemporary American Horror Fiction
Contemporary American Literary Theory
Contemporary American Science Fiction, 1926–1970
Contemporary American Science Fiction, 1970–2000
Contemporary Chicana Literature | Robert Coover | Philip K. Dick
James Dickey | E. L. Doctorow | Rita Dove | John Gardner | George Garrett
Tim Gautreaux | John Hawkes | Joseph Heller | Lillian Hellman | Beth Henley
James Leo Herlihy | David Henry Hwang | John Irving | Randall Jarrell
Charles Johnson | Diane Johnson | Adrienne Kennedy | William Kennedy
Jack Kerouac | Jamaica Kincaid | Etheridge Knight | Tony Kushner
Ursula K. Le Guin | Denise Levertov | Bernard Malamud | David Mamet
Bobbie Ann Mason | Colum McCann | Cormac McCarthy | Jill McCorkle
Carson McCullers | W. S. Merwin | Arthur Miller | Stephen Millhauser
Lorrie Moore | Toni Morrison's Fiction | Vladimir Nabokov | Gloria Naylor
Joyce Carol Oates | Tim O'Brien | Flannery O'Connor | Cynthia Ozick
Suzan-Lori Parks | Walker Percy | Katherine Anne Porter | Richard Powers
Reynolds Price | Annie Proulx | Thomas Pynchon | Theodore Roethke
Philip Roth | May Sarton | Hubert Selby, Jr. | Mary Lee Settle | Sam Shepard
Neil Simon | Isaac Bashevis Singer | Jane Smiley | Gary Snyder | William Stafford
Robert Stone | Anne Tyler | Gerald Vizenor | Kurt Vonnegut
David Foster Wallace | Robert Penn Warren | James Welch | Eudora Welty
Edmund White | Tennessee Williams | August Wilson | Charles Wright

UNDERSTANDING

MICHAEL CHABON

Joseph Dewey

The University of South Carolina Press

Published by the University of South Carolina Press
Columbia, South Carolina 29208

www.sc.edu/uscpress

Manufactured in the United States of America

23 22 21 20 19 18 17 16 15 14   10 9 8 7 6 5 4 3 2 1

Library of Congress Cataloging-in-Publication Data

Dewey, Joseph.
Understanding Michael Chabon / Joseph Dewey.
pages cm. — (Understanding Contemporary American Literature)
Includes bibliographical references and index.
ISBN 978-1-61117-339-0 (hardbound : alk. paper) — ISBN 978-1-61117-340-6 (e-book) 1. Chabon, Michael—Criticism and interpretation. I. Title.
PS3553.H15Z69 2014
813'.54—dc23

2013032138

This book was printed on a recycled paper with 30 percent postconsumer waste content.

CONTENTS

SERIES EDITOR'S PREFACE

The Understanding Contemporary American Literature series was founded by the estimable Matthew J. Bruccoli (1931–2008), who envisioned these volumes as guides or companions for students as well as good nonacademic readers, a legacy that will continue as new volumes are developed to fill in gaps among the nearly one hundred series volumes published to date and to embrace a host of new writers only now making their marks on our literature.

As Professor Bruccoli explained in his preface to the volumes he edited, because much influential contemporary literature makes special demands, "the word understanding in the titles was chosen deliberately. Many willing readers lack an adequate understanding of how contemporary literature works; that is, of what the author is attempting to express and the means by which it is conveyed." Aimed at fostering this understanding of good literature and good writers, the criticism and analysis in the series provide instruction in how to read certain contemporary writers—explicating their material, language, structures, themes, and perspectives—and facilitate a more profitable experience of the works under discussion.

In the twenty-first century Professor Bruccoli's prescience gives us an avenue to publish expert critiques of significant contemporary American writing. The series continues to map the literary landscape and to provide both instruction and enjoyment. Future volumes will seek to introduce new voices alongside canonized favorites, to chronicle the changing literature of our times, and to remain, as Professor Bruccoli conceived, contemporary in the best sense of the word.

Linda Wagner-Martin, Series Editor

ACKNOWLEDGMENTS

There are several people who have been instrumental in completing this writing project. First I would like to thank Jay Parini of Middlebury College who, more than fifteen years ago, through his editorship of the Scribner American Writers series, first introduced me to the wonder and power of Chabon's fiction. In addition I would like to thank Michael Cocchiarale (Widener University) and Scott D. Emmert (University of Wisconsin), who invited me to submit a reading of *Summerland* for their volume on sports fiction for the Critical Insights series (EBSCO). Although that reading went in a considerably different direction from the one presented here, both Michael and Scott offered helpful responses to my evolving reading of Chabon's fantasy baseball novel. I would also like to thank Michael Chabon's father, Dr. Robert S. Chabon, who graciously fielded a number of my no doubt intrusive email queries. And I would be remiss if I did not thank Chabon himself, who not only produced these marvelous fictions but who happily participated in an email exchange that helped shape the focus of the present study and encouraged me beyond words.

On a more personal level, I would like to thank my wife, Julie, who not only allowed me the time to work out this reading upstairs, where I was for more than a year in the computer than at the computer, but who, as the administrative assistant for the University of Pittsburgh Library System, was instrumental in helping me acquire a wide variety of materials, both in print and online, quickly and easily. I would like to thank my son, Mark, a computer software engineer, who patiently guided me through a number of computer near-catastrophes and kept the writing project on schedule and indeed saved me enormous time and trouble. And my daughter, Carolyn, and her husband, Andy, who in the middle of the writing of this study gifted us with our first grandchild, the pixieish Annabelle. Her easy laugh and impish smile showed me at a pivotal moment in the project the tender wisdom of Chabon's generous and compassionate humanism.

CHAPTER 1

Understanding Michael Chabon

> The imagination is the expression of a yearning that a few magic words and an artful hand might produce something—one poor, dumb, powerful thing—exempt from the crushing strictures, from the ills, cruelties and inevitable failures of the greater Creation.
>
> Michael Chabon, *Kavalier & Clay*, p. 582

Nightly, under a tented blanket, a twelve-year-old Michael Chabon pored over a heavily creased map—one of those brightly colored cartoon souvenir maps that Disney distributes to its Orlando visitors to help them navigate the often baffling walkways of its magical kingdoms. Michael had brought the map back to his Maryland home from what would turn out to be his family's last vacation together, an excursion to the newly opened Magic Kingdom in Walt Disney World. Even as his parents' marriage did its torturously slow-motion crash and burn into the apparently irrevocable sundering of divorce, the boy would be sustained by plotting an imaginary escape into a furtive magic kingdom of his own devising, an elaborate underground world of passageways latticed beneath Disney's massive theme park. "I figured I could sleep during the daytime, in some forgotten garret of Cinderella's Castle [*sic*] or in the tangled and artificial wilderness of Tom Sawyer's Island, emerging at night to melt into the crowd, picking pockets and rifling handbags left unattended, feasting endlessly on frozen bananas and French fries." As young Michael conceived it, that subterranean refuge could shelter other desperate children "hidden in the corners and stairwells and leafy shadows of Disney World"; children similarly blindsided by the unexpected; despite their tender years, children already nostalgic; children who had learned that the best times had somehow already passed and who now needed a refuge safe from the "grim-faced men . . . who carried walkie-talkies and did not wear name tags" ("Disney of the Mind"). The critical element of this adolescent fantasy would surely be familiar to readers of the bittersweet fictions of the grown-up Michael Chabon: the anxious tension between escape and engagement, between the sweet, centripetal pull of the imagination and the harsh, centrifugal pull of real life.

Since the publication of his first novel in 1988, Michael Chabon has moved to the forefront of the post-Pynchon era, writers born after 1960—among them Jennifer Egan, Nathan Englander, Jeffrey Eugenides, Jonathan Safran Foer, Jonathan Franzen, Rick Moody, Richard Powers, Elizabeth Strout—who are in many ways the first generation of American writers produced almost entirely by universities, specifically by creative writing programs. As fledgling writers in university classrooms, they traded the easy charm of reading books and the coaxing pull of story and character for the intellectual rigors of analyzing texts. They studied dense avant-garde postmodern theories about narrative de/reconstruction, fashionable theories that questioned the very legitimacy of language and the viability of the reading act they had each loved since childhood. But these writers, call them post-postmodernists, alarmed by the dead-end implications of de/reconstructing books into language experiments, sought to restore narrative to a balance, producing serious fictions that maintain the intellectual reach of formal experimentation, certainly, but reclaim as well the inviting imperative of storytelling. Their narratives perceive the reader not as a shadowy antagonist in some elaborate chess match but as a friend, indeed a necessary element of the storytelling dynamic. As Chabon pointed out to me in a 2012 email exchange, "I want my sentences to climb high, dive deep . . . but I will always put my hand out to the reader, to say, 'Come with me'—not because I want to be pursued or shadowed but because I sincerely want the company. Literature to me—pre-and post-Pynchon—is a partnership between reader and writer, a game played by equals, not to ensure one's victory and the other's corresponding loss but simply and purely for the pleasure to be had therein."

In short, these post-postmodern writers, most prominent among them Chabon, deliberately brought together the defining elements of the two principal expressions of the American narrative at mid-century: the formal extravagances of the postmodern era and the compelling consolations of old school storytelling. Like the postmodern excesses and self-conscious audacities of Pynchon and his disciples, Chabon's fictions have been extravagant experiments in form (testing particularly the dynamics of narrative voice); they have been playful, self-conscious investigations in reanimating traditional genres; they have been executed in a lyric prose that often dazzles with its density and its kinetics, foregrounding, in the best postmodern tradition, the author's nimble dexterity with language. But like the probing texts of psychological realism of John Updike and his disciples, Chabon's fictions have developed recognizable characters caught up in recognizable (and often heartbreaking) dilemmas and enthralling storylines compelled by suspense, enriched with suggestive symbols, and working toward humane insights into love and death, work and family. Across four decades now, Chabon's writings—novels, short stories, and a growing body of engaging essays (by any measure a most prolific output)—have become a staple in both high school and university syllabi. He has been consistently praised by reviewers and sought out by interviewers. He has been listed by both the *New Yorker* and *Granta* as among the most important writers of his generation. His books, despite the "stigma" of being serious fiction, have maintained a regular presence on best-seller lists and several of his titles have been optioned as big-budget film projects. He has been feted with prestigious awards, most notably an O. Henry Award for best short fiction (1999), a Nebula Award for Best Novel in science fiction (2007), a Hugo Award for Best Novel in science fiction or fantasy (2008), and the Pulitzer Prize for Fiction (2001). In late 2011 he was selected to chair the board of directors of MacDowell Colony in Peterborough, New Hampshire, for more than a century one of the most prominent and influential retreats for young American writers and artists. In 2012, though only in his forties, Chabon was elected to the American Academy of Arts and Letters, an august and exclusive body (250 members) comprised of the most respected figures in contemporary literature, fine arts, and music.

Yet the critical establishment has been cautious. Perhaps it was wary over Chabon's notable success in the marketplace or of his singular accessibility or of his celebrity good looks—early in his career, he was "honored" in one of *People* magazine's annual listings of the country's Most Beautiful People—or perhaps it was skeptical of his remarkable productivity in an era where his contemporaries would routinely publish a book a decade. Or perhaps some critics were put off by his eager willingness to expand his narrative range into comic books, television, and film or by his stylish explorations of narrative genres long associated with low- octane pop culture (the detective story, sci-fi, fantasy, horror stories, sports fiction, comic books, adventure serials). The critical establishment initially investigated Chabon only in the limited scope of largely laudatory reviews and the occasional mention in journal articles.[1] The 2000 publication of the Pulitzer Prize–winning *The Amazing Adventures of Kavalier & Clay*, however, generated a much wider interest in Chabon, although that attention largely focused on the emerging debate over exactly how Jewish Chabon was, a rather narrow angle that Chabon himself has positioned as important, certainly, but not critical to understanding his narrative sensibility. His interest is far more ingrained in a much broader investigation of the American narrative. Despite producing a body of defiantly hip work that confidently explores (and ultimately challenges) contemporary notions of narrative, Chabon's fictional sensibility is firmly centered on what has been the defining theme of American literature since Hawthorne's tragicomic Surveyor, the restless Tramp-Narrator of Thoreau's *Walden,* Melville's pale-skinned Sub-Sub Librarian, and Emily Dickinson's Wounded Child: namely, the scope, breadth, and scale of the imagination. More specifically this treats the anxious tension between escape and engagement, between the sweet, centripetal pull of the redemptive imagination—a splendid, if imperfect, engine of retreat capable of shaping the most elegant and suasive artifacts—and the harsh, centrifugal pull of real life, which is recklessly deformed by the crude handiwork of surprise and chance and unable to coax even the simplest appearance of logic.

Chabon's defining characters are book-fed and word-fat, inveterate readers, wounded writers, self-conscious storytellers, articulate talkers, sustained performance pieces, and/or consummate liars. Curmudgeonly recluses, they haunt claustrophobic shelter-environments, barricaded far from the devastating conflicts and slow-burn agonies of the real world. They hide out in universities; in the foggy non-space of drugs and alcohol abuse; in second-hand stores well off the beaten track; in tricked-out basements and canopic libraries; in the tidy game-world of sports (most notably chess and baseball); in generously beaten-up cars, long-forgotten hidden tunnels, garages, extravagantly outfitted bedrooms, even coffins. His characters are gifted and cursed with vivid and potent imaginations, willingly conjuring convincing edifice-worlds from the accommodating availability of words, fashioning protective bunkers that provide them each with soft and coaxing prisons. To justify such protective retreats, however, Chabon proffers a most unsettling vision of the late twentieth century, a world defined by the emotional terrorism implicit in love's cycle of expectation and disappointment. This involves the shadowy intrusion of mortality; the clumsy interference of bad luck and the fist-blow of surprise; the pervasive reach of greed; the peculiar woundings exacted by family; the blind clumsy handiwork of genetics; the irresistible itch of sexual attraction and the anxious confusions generated by its unpredictable appetites; the inevitability of betrayal by friends and lovers; and ultimately the heavy burden of loneliness. Buffeted, Chabon's characters seek shelter.

Although one risks simplification to extract from a single traumatic childhood experience the protocols of a future writer, Chabon himself has recalled a particularly unsettling experience in June 1972, when he was nine. Hurricane Agnes, a freak early summer storm cell, inelegantly and improbably came roaring up the East Coast and drew a clear bead on the Washington, D.C./Maryland enclave where Chabon's family lived, "raising river and drowning railroads and knocking out power all over the D.C. area" (*Manhood for Amateurs* 208). Staying that week with his grandparents in Silver Spring, Maryland, while contractors put finishing touches on his family's new home in nearby Columbia, young Michael was sent to the basement for his safety. There he would spend an interminable night fearing the imminent inrush of what he imagined was a black wall of swirling flood waters—but what Chabon recalled years later was the protective feel of the basement itself, literally a shelter from the storm. It had a most tonic effect on the boy. "I suppose it is no accident that basements, hidden lairs, and underground settings have featured so routinely in my fiction. . . . You can find buried treasuries, Batcaves and hidey-holes, half-forgotten underground worlds that perhaps encode the rapture and the bitterness of my own isolation" (*Manhood for Amateurs* 209).

Indeed Chabon's characters are shelter-dwellers, victims of brutal surprise and inelegant shocks that reveal the hard vulnerability of those who lack the protective insulation of the imagination. In his fictions, a child drowns; a young parent drops dead; apparently stable marriages implode into divorce; passion stales like bread left out overnight; a lover betrays the simplest promise of fidelity; a car suddenly veers off a road; the hard-wiring of genetics inexplicably plays a ghastly trick on an unborn child; work flatlines into routine; casual lovers confront an unwanted pregnancy; long-suffering would-be parents cannot turn the trick of conception; death intrudes, always premature, always absolute. Like the adolescent Chabon seeking the quiet calm of the basement-fortress against that frightening storm or handling there under a tented blanket in his bedroom the imminent approach of his parents' divorce by constructing a perfect magic kingdom, these characters, reeling from the brutal intrusion of surprise, take refuge in protective spaces fashioned by the energy of the imagination. They exist within a complicated either-or dilemma: either indulge elegant private magic kingdoms or accept being ordinary, left naked amid sheer event. As the adolescent Chabon surely intuited there beneath the tented blanket, his flashlight precariously illuminating a world he coaxed into being, any magic kingdom he could conjure would be abundantly more attractive than his own home that was so inelegantly collapsing all about him into rubble. The adult Chabon, however, recognized the impossibility of such refuge and, ultimately, cannot endorse the coaxing lure of the imagination and its intriguing retreat. But the Chabon characters who come to realize the danger in retreat are often leveled by such revelations: they commit suicide; they disappear into addictions; they fall back into heavy indifference; they turn into misanthropic recluses, living suicides, surrendered, joyless, alone. Only the rare Chabon character, rocked by events and their unpredictability, comes to accept the imperfect world, its brutalities and its wonders. Chabon has drawn on his Jewish heritage to offer as examples of courageous engagement with a harsh world the European Jewry during the long night of Hitler's Holocaust and, further back, the ancient Jews commemorated by the celebration of Passover, the holy days that recall the Jews' dignity and triumph amid intolerable conditions of enslavement and against the horrific threat of ethnic cleansing. That willingness to embrace the dark chaos of existence, to accept vulnerability not as a weakness but as a strength, marks the heroic characters in Chabon's fiction.

Born too late to experience firsthand the existential suburban angst of the gray-flannel Eisenhower boom or to fathom the bloody civics lesson delivered in the streets of urban America during the 1960s or to participate in the flamboyant (melo)drama of the Woodstock counterculture, Chabon instead grew up in the loopy, often foggy, freedom of the mid-1970s, in the spacious unease of post-Vietnam, post-Watergate America. "What happened in the seventies was that, as at no other time before or since in our history, Americans . . . were, for better and worse, free. Liberated, we cast aside the laws and limitations of the old familiar system to sail like *Voyager* out into the interstellar medium beyond" (*Manhood for Amateurs* 202). But freedom, as Chabon would testify in the fictions he later created, can be both exhilarating and terrifying. His are compassionate fictions of characters that undergo dramatic moments of interior shattering and who gain often unflattering insight into the nature of their own dilemmas. Like that young boy poring over the theme-park map, such characters must then sort from among the possible responses to such mysteries and sorrows the decidedly human mess of the late twentieth century. Some escape from its brutality via the imagination; others surrender sourly to its banality; and there are the rare, privileged few who, relishing the logic of the imagination, come as well to exalt in the real world's manifest imperfections.

Michael William Chabon (pronounced "shay" as in Shea Stadium, "bahn" as in Bon Jovi, as he was fond of telling interviewers early in his career) was born May 24, 1963, in Georgetown University Hospital in Washington, D.C.[2] At the time his father, Robert S. Chabon, born and raised in the working-class Jewish neighborhoods of Brooklyn, New York, was just completing his M.D. at Georgetown. His mother, born Sharon Cohen, a native of Richmond, Virginia, ran the house. Over the next several years Dr. Chabon would begin a successful pediatrics practice with the Public Health Service, a massive government agency of more than 6,000 doctors and nurses headquartered in nearby Washington and dedicated to disseminating information to advance health and safety practices and to promote disease reduction, particularly in urban areas. In 1969, Chabon's parents secured a housing loan through the Veterans Administration (Dr. Chabon had served a stint in the Coast Guard) and moved the family—Michael and Stephen, his younger brother by five years—to Columbia, Maryland, a planned community of nearly 14,000 acres located nearly midway between Baltimore and Washington. To borrow from the Disney conceptual, this real-life Experimental Prototype Community of Tomorrow had been launched two years earlier by urban visionaries, led by Maryland real estate millionaire James Rouse, intent on creating a kind of theme park-qua-city, an idyllic predesigned suburban utopia with a classic small-town community feel. The Chabons, along with the hundreds of other forward-thinking families moving into the new homes, were considered pioneers, first-generation settlers in a radical experiment in urban planning. Their self-contained model city, actually a dozen smaller towns grouped about a kind of hub, was built from scratch complete with new schools, hospitals, churches, and shops, its socio-economic makeup carefully balanced to maintain diversity. The prefabricated city was also free from the characteristic blight and deteriorating infrastructure of the older metropolitan areas up and down the East Coast corridor. As Chabon recalled years later, "[These families] were colonists of a dream, immigrants to a new land that as yet existed mostly on paper" (*Maps and Legends* 27). The Chabons had in fact moved into a kind of virtual city. In 1969 Columbia, Maryland, was less a real place than an exotic (and for some controversial) theory in urban socioeconomic engineering whose reality was largely confined to enthusiastic promotional pamphlets and ambitious architectural blueprints. As the city evolved during Chabon's childhood, its aggressive public-relations promoters trumpeted Columbia's virtues: negligible crime rate; inviting streets, impeccably manicured park-swatches; tidy model homes; efficient traffic management; and supremely blue-ribbon school systems.

Raised within such a model world, the socially awkward Michael (a geek, by his own admission) turned early on, perhaps inevitably, to easy escape into the colorful panel-world of comic books. His paternal grandfather had been a career typographer at a printing plant in Manhattan's West Side and had regularly sent bags of old comics to Michael's father, which the doctor in turn presented to his oldest son. As Michael's interest broadened, his father frequently purchased newer, cutting-edge comics, which his son devoured. For a man born in the latter years of the Depression and raised to abide by the old-school family dynamic in which the father was the breadwinner and was not expected to give in to showy demonstrations of touchy-feely emotion, the gift of the comic books demonstrated the deep affection Dr. Chabon had for his older son. Michael was so clearly engaged by the fetching primary-color world of comic books, their caricature villains, their larger-than-life heroes, and their high-octane, perpetual-motion crises that inevitably pitted recognizable Good against recognizable Evil. But what Dr. Chabon did not suspect was that Michael was most enthralled with the storytelling, the exertion of the imagination into vivid and rollicking plots. By early adolescence, Michael was a voracious reader—indeed, once a week for years Dr. Chabon would drive Michael to the community's public library to secure a new pile of books. Each one, whether adventure stories or mysteries or horror tales, offered a most inviting and welcoming safe-house for a child not given easily to social interactions. For years young Michael sustained the consolations of an imaginary friend, named Cheyenne, who still, nearly forty years later, stirred in him a "golden something, always nearby," as Chabon recounted to me in an email exchange.

That would indeed become something of a pattern for Chabon as a child: the casual shuttle between reality and created worlds. In addition to reading, for instance, he relished the architectural license (and monkish solitude) of constructing Legos, stacking the boldly colored blocks into complex forms that, unlike boxed puzzles or airplane models, gave him the freedom to create shapes and to push his imaginative energy into original constructions. There was something hypnotic, intriguing about such creativity, and he invented stories to go along with the creatures and objects he designed. And there was, improbably enough, his interest in cooking. Before he was ten, Michael became enamored with the creative processes in the kitchen—his prized gift on his eleventh birthday was an encyclopedic cookbook. He delighted not only in following the tidiness of his mother's handwritten recipe cards (in their own way, little model worlds, blueprints for efficient constructions) but enjoyed as well the opportunities to ad-lib during meal preparation, which he did largely on his own with only the loosest supervision from his mother, finding in cooking the same creative release he had found in comic books and Legos. But above all he discovered the pleasure of storytelling. At five Michael was already experimenting with telling and even writing stories—at ten he garnered praise from his English teacher with the first story he shared in school, "The Revenge of Captain Nemo," a wildly imaginative tale centered on a dialogue between two fictional characters who had long fascinated him: Jules Verne's mysterious recluse Captain Nemo and Conan Doyle's master detective Sherlock Holmes. The story, which he wrote with painstaking care on his mother's electric typewriter, was actually rendered in a careful impersonation of the rich Anglo-Saxon diction of Dr. Watson, a significant challenge for a ten-year-old. In twelfth grade, Michael received a dictionary as first prize in a story-writing contest. Years later, Chabon credited that dictionary for developing his love of exotic vocabulary and his evolution into appreciating the sheer sonic appeal of words. Forty years later, he still uses the same well-thumbed dictionary as a critical writing tool. By early adolescence, Michael was sure he would write stories for a living. Far from discouraging such an eccentric decision, his parents encouraged their older son's interest.

But Michael's giddy love of comic books, his nerdy fascination with the original architectures of Legos, his joyful labors in the kitchen, even his easy retreat into the imaginative playscapes of his own stories were all tempered against a steadily accumulating series of emotional traumas. This complex dynamic shaped what would become the adult Chabon's centering theme: the tension between the difficult engagement of a hard and bruising reality and the sweet escape of the imagination. Although young Michael struggled at sports (by early adolescence he was pudgy and sported dorky aviator glasses), he was a baseball junkie (and would be until 2007 when in disgust over the controversial asterisked ascent of Giants slugger Barry Bonds to baseball's all-time home run leader, he reluctantly turned his back on the game he loved). Two critical events constellated the baseball recollections from his childhood. When he was an eight-year-old, the abrupt decision was announced in late September, 1971, to relocate his beloved Washington Senators (perennial losers, yes, but his team nevertheless) to Arlington, Texas, a place so distant, so remote it might as well have been another galaxy. After reluctantly switching his tender allegiances to the far more successful Pittsburgh Pirates, he heard on the radio on New Year's Day two years later that his new hero, Roberto Clemente, the team's clutch power hitter and charismatic right fielder, had been killed. His chartered plane delivering relief supplies for victims of a devastating earthquake in Nicaragua had crashed into the Pacific. These are not, of course, a child's normal baseball recollections, typically warm, fuzzy memories with reassuringly easy lessons about never giving up or keeping your eye on the ball or how winning isn't everything. Rather, a very young Michael learned very adult lessons about abrupt and intrusive change and the consequent feeling of helplessness; about vulnerability and the awful crush of disappointment; about the difficult reality of loss and the devastating hammer stroke of mortality; and the need for haphazard improvisation amid the wide energy field of contingency and against the threat of the vertiginous drop, much like that doomed rescue plane, into an absolute and unforgiving nothingness.

But undoubtedly the centering trauma of Chabon's childhood was his parents' divorce in 1975, a family crisis, he would recall years later, that caused him, at the age of twelve, anxieties he never felt comfortable broaching aloud, certain that the obligation of being the older son was to maintain the superstructure of the family in the sudden, graceless absence of the father. After the divorce Dr. Chabon, who had just completed a law degree from the University of Maryland, relocated to Pittsburgh, where he practiced pediatrics and taught as an adjunct professor at the Duquesne University School of Law before embarking on a thirty-year career as a lawyer and hospital administrator. (Now past seventy, Dr. Chabon currently serves as legal counsel for a prestigious Washington, D.C., law firm that specializes in malpractice suits). For most of his adolescence, Chabon summered in Pittsburgh and visited there for holidays—his younger brother moved there to live with their father and his new wife in 1976. After the divorce, Michael's mother returned to school. By the time Michael turned fourteen in 1977, she had completed a law degree from the University of Baltimore and then accepted what would become a career position at a federal agency in Washington.

For his part, with his brother gone and his mother working long days (and taking up again the awkward negotiations of dating), Michael fell back on his own resources with limited success. He gained weight, developed terrible acne, and indulged a nervous habit of nearly continuously gnawing on his fingernails. However, he also greatly expanded his aesthetic reach—buffeted, he sought shelters. Abandoning comic books as too juvenile early in high school, he tapped into an increasingly wider range of imaginative expressions: the comic films of Woody Allen, which positioned the timid, ineffectual nebbish as hero; the avant-garde satire and inspired silliness of the British television comedy troupe Monty Python; the irreverent and often sophomoric humor of *MAD* magazine; the creepy, off-the-wall tales of H. P. Lovecraft, an obscure and decidedly eccentric early twentieth-century American writer of horror and weird fiction often eclipsed by the considerable shadow of Edgar Allan Poe; the splashy spectacle concert-events and arena anthems of artsy British prog-rock bands such as Yes and Queen, King Crimson and Genesis; the unrepentantly misogynistic underground soft porn of Henry Miller; the panoramic breadth and wild imaginary landscapes of J. R. R. Tolkien's *Lord of the Rings* trilogy; and the daring of science fiction, most notably the sprawling *Ringworld* cycle of Larry Niven and the bleak, dystopian fictions of J. G. Ballard. In retreating into such a stunning variety of entirely symbolic playscapes, model worlds of fiction, film, music, and television, Michael, wounded by the deep trauma of his parents' divorce, sought stability, a reassuring shelter, what he would later describe as a search for a "home, a world to call my own" (*Maps and Legends* 170).

A gifted, if quiet, student in high school, Chabon matriculated at Pittsburgh's prestigious Carnegie Mellon University, then as now known internationally for its cutting-edge curricula in the sciences and technology. But for a kid who dreamed of telling stories, it was at best an awkward fit. After one term, Chabon transferred across town to the University Pittsburgh where he began to study literature in earnest, completing an English degree in 1984. Now feeling liberated and free to embrace his deep love of literature at Pitt, Chabon blossomed, shedding his baby fat, developing myriad friendships, and experimenting in the typical rebellions of upper-class, white, suburban college kids in the era: sex (a series of lovers that introduced him to the wonder and complexities of physical love), drugs (mostly the mellow retreat of marijuana), and rock and roll (most notably discovering the anarchic alternative-rock band Big Star). During his junior year, Chabon, not gifted with the command of any musical instrument, sang lead in a short-lived pseudo-punk-ish garage band known as the Bats. But Chabon chiefly read, widely and voraciously—most indelibly, William Faulkner, Raymond Chandler, Jorge Luis Borges, Donald Barthelme, and Frank O'Hara—all the while honing his command of the story-writing craft. During his junior and senior years, he edited the university's student literary magazine. As he entered his senior year, he was determined to become a writer rather than pursuing, as most of his friends planned, an academic career as a scholar/teacher. After graduation, with his mother now remarried to an optometrist and living in the Bay Area of Oakland, California, Chabon headed across country, enrolling in the M.F.A. program at the University of California at Irvine. Despite the you're-not-in-Kansas-anymore exotic feel of Southern California, he found in the company of other fledgling student writers, and under the tutelage of the school's faculty, critical emotional support and encouragement.

Initially Chabon lived in the basement of his mother's home in Oakland. Even as he began taking his graduate classes in the architecture of fiction and the dynamics of narrative, he pondered the challenge of writing a novel. After all, it seemed that all the other Master's candidates were engaged in just such an ambitious enterprise. To that point, Chabon had worked solely in short fiction. "Was everyone obligated to write a novel? Could I write a novel? Did I want to write a novel? What the hell was a novel anyway, when you came right down to it? A really, really, really long short story?" (*Maps and Legends* 147). He began with a single, striking (admittedly autobiographical) image—a twenty-something, angst-ridden man-child with a freshly-minted college degree, his life's direction now decidedly uncertain, contemplating the steady and unerring flow of traffic along a city street. The image would over several months evolve into a novel-length narrative, a bittersweet coming-of-age story, set in Pittsburgh, about an economics major during the summer after his college graduation. It would become Chabon's master's thesis. In the narrative, clearly influenced by Chabon's admiration for F. Scott Fitzgerald's *The Great Gatsby,* Art Bechstein, the son of a powerful Jewish gangster, struggles to come to terms with his father and his ties to the Baltimore mob as well as with his own sexual identity. He is tested by two summer-long affairs, one a conventional postgraduation romance with a gorgeous, if demanding, librarian and the other a far less conventional relationship with a street-wise, ultra-hip gay man, an intern at the university library and a professional house-sitter, whose trenchant wit and taste for exotica give Art's summer a dangerous depth and unexpected vitality. One of Chabon's professors, writer MacDonald Harris (the pseudonym of Donald Heiney), greatly admired the work. Without Chabon's knowledge, Harris forwarded the completed thesis to a New York literary agent who immediately sensed its merit and its commercial possibilities and negotiated a staggering advance of $155,000 at a time when advances for first-time novelists were far more modest, usually a few thousand dollars.

In the summer of 1987, shortly before the novel was scheduled to be released, Chabon married Iola (Lollie) Groth, seven years his senior, an aspiring poet and Ph.D. candidate he had met at Irvine. They were married at her family's farm outside Seattle. By temperament, Groth at the time was melancholic, moody, struggling to find her poetic voice, torn by the practical demands of career and the daunting prospects for market success as a poet. "She had an eye for furniture and flowers, a rich history of weird sex, weird jobs, and weird scenes, an ear for quirky pop tunes. I found that you could make her intensely happy for a little while with a handful of sweet peas or by putting her in a dinghy and handing her a pair of good binoculars and sending her out very early to row softly among the coots and the buffetheads" (*Manhood for Amateurs* 115). But events would move quickly for the newly married Chabon. Published to glowing reviews in 1988 and hyped by his publisher as a new generation's *Catcher in the Rye, The Mysteries of Pittsburgh* became that rare combination: a work of serious fiction that sells. So authentic was Chabon's depiction of Art's sexual conflict that Chabon, himself heterosexual (although he had had a sexual relationship with a man while at Pitt), was hailed at the time by *Newsweek* magazine as one of America's most promising gay novelists. Chabon was flattered. He later told *Rolling Stone,* "I'm interested in questions of identity and sexuality and how things like that get determined and defined. And I'm interested especially in relationships between straight men and gay men, because I think there are a lot of friendships like that out there where one best friend is gay and one is straight, but those friendships I don't think get written about much, or depicted or portrayed in movies and television" (Binelli 78).

Almost literally Chabon had become an overnight sensation, a wunderkind, a wonder boy. His celebrity was helped by his striking good looks, his unaffected cool charisma, his affable and approachable personality (despite his natural shyness), and his easy accessibility with interviewers and readers alike at a time when writers of serious fiction more often adapted surly personas that valued hip postures of seclusion and disdained market embrace. At twenty-four Chabon enjoyed the sort of prominence rookie novelists only dream about (including the flattering offer from *People* magazine and an invitation to serve as spokesperson in national commercials for the trendy clothing chain The Gap, both of which Chabon politely refused). And he received a much-publicized hefty advance for his sophomore effort, which was unspecified at the time. That advance, however, began what would turn into a slow-motion debacle, both private and professional, a disheartening struggle with an exponentially expanding manuscript about an oddball architect who conceives of constructing a perfect baseball park. As if writing themselves, the story's plotlines expanded into myriads of alternate narratives and introduced casts of new characters, each bringing new backstories. After two years, Chabon felt the project start to slip out of his control. The manuscript, which he had titled "Fountain City," would obsess Chabon for more than five years, eventually accumulating to more than one thousand single-spaced pages. He quickly lost confidence in himself, fearing that he was nothing more than a one-book wonder. His marriage suffered. Indeed he and Lollie divorced in 1990, "[Lollie] was often miserable—sometimes justifiably, usually for no reason at all—and in a short period of time, I found that I was miserable, too. There were operatic arguments, all-night ransackings of the contents of our souls, drunken vituperations, migraines, rages, grim gray bitter mornings" (*Manhood for Amateurs* 115). After the couple separated, Chabon adopted something of a self-destructive, peripatetic lifestyle as he struggled with the manuscript, moving seven times in just under four years including stays in Key West, Seattle, and San Francisco. He did continue to publish a steady stream of elegant and much admired short fiction, many in the *New Yorker*—most notably five stories about an impressionable young boy whose parents divorce, gathered in what Chabon called *The Lost World* cycle. But "Fountain City" eluded his control. Reluctantly, after returning to Southern California in 1993, he abandoned the manuscript project altogether. Long afterward, in 2010, he published four heavily annotated chapter fragments from the manuscript on his website as a way to illustrate the frenetic energy of the undisciplined creative process.

The decision to abandon "Fountain City," as wrenching and as painful as it was, would in retrospect come to mark a kind of positive turning point or Chabon. In October 1993, after a whirlwind courtship, he married Ayelet Waldman, an aspiring writer who was at the time pursuing a law degree. They had met on a blind date in New York City—Waldman had never heard of Chabon and after a quick read of *The Mysteries of Pittsburgh* and some of his *New Yorker* stories had assumed her blind date was gay. What they discovered, however, was a deep and abiding love the likes of which Chabon later claimed testified to the authenticity of what he had spent his life just reading about. They married in a public ceremony in a city park in Berkeley. But Chabon still agonized over the abandoned novel. In that same year, Ayelet informed Chabon that she intended to focus on passing the bar, a demanding regimen that would consume her time and energies for several months. With Ayelet focused on the bar exam, Chabon decided to use the time to redirect his creative energies into a new project, inspired as much by the lengthy and demoralizing frustrations of "Fountain City" as by an unexpected epiphanic moment when a single, stark image had struck him: a young man standing in the deep shadows of a driveway holding a cartoonishly tiny silver pistol in his steady hand. Who was he? Why the silver pistol? As the storyline began to reveal itself, Chabon could see it would be a much less ambitious narrative than the sprawling maximalist "Fountain City." Instead it became the intimate story of a burned-out writer, lost within an unfinishable manuscript, who was marking time as a creative- writing professor in a small college. Quickly Chabon regained his narrative confidence. Within a breathless seven months, Chabon delivered to his publishers his long-promised second novel, titled *Wonder Boys,* a comic romp about the mentor-disciple relationship between that frustrated writer and one of his more promising writing students (the kid with the pistol). It contained a coming-of-age narrative that depicted as well, with generous poignancy, the serious silliness of college—its pretentious faculty, its supercilious administrators, its all-too-tragic students—all set in the familiar environs of Chabon's Pittsburgh.

Published in 1995, the novel tracked the outrageous events of a single turning-point weekend in the slow-motion midlife crisis of Grady Tripp, the frustrated novelist-turned-faux-professor, a fortyish alcoholic pothead and serial philanderer. Tripp must suddenly confront not only the abrupt departure of his wife (his third) after she discovers his current infidelity but also the unexpected pregnancy of his current mistress, who happens to be the dean of his college and, incidentally, the wife of his boss, the department chair. The audacious plotline involves, among other things, a stolen evening jacket once owned by Marilyn Monroe, a dead blind malamute, a heisted car, a gorgeous transvestite, a tuba, and several feet of a crushed boa constrictor. The novel moved with flair and surety and garnered for Chabon immediate critical plaudits as a comic tour de force. However Chabon, perhaps smarting from the unsettling experience of "Fountain City," saw the character of a terminally blocked middle-aged writer more cautionary than amusing. Given its cinematic sense of scene, perfectly calibrated street-sharp dialogue, bittersweet comedy, marvelous cast of immediately engaging characters, spot-on lampoon of the eccentricities of both the university life and the publishing world, choreographed indulgence of broad slapstick, and its un-ironically Capraesque happy ending, the novel sold well and was quickly optioned for the movies. The 2000 Paramount film, an intelligent and savvy adaptation directed by Curtis Hanson (*L.A. Confidential; 8 Miles; The Hand That Rocks the Cradle*) and starring Michael Douglas as Grady Tripp, fared indifferently at the box office but revived respectably as a video rental.

The completion of *Wonder Boys,* and its success, quashed Chabon's darkling fears about his own talent. In June 1999, the *New Yorker* listed Chabon among the twenty best American writers under forty. His domestic life in Southern California flourished, giving him the grounding, the home, he had long sought. Ayelet completed her law degree and worked as a federal public defender but, disillusioned, left the justice system altogether to pursue her own writing career. She would pen a series of popular mysteries and maintain a much-visited blog in which she discussed candidly her personal life, most notably her struggle with bipolar disorder. The couple had four children: Sophie, Ezekiel, Ida-Rose, and Abraham. A fifth, whom Chabon poignantly named Rocketship, was lost in miscarriage, a devastating event he would treat only years later in *The Yiddish Policemen's Union.* Under the potent influence of his family and the unaffected joy he took in the day-to-day delights and anxieties of being very much a hands-on father, Chabon came to reconnect as well with his Jewish roots. (His first wife was not Jewish and during the difficult struggles with his aborted novel he had drifted from his Jewish identity. Ayelet, by contrast, had been born in Jerusalem and her religion was very much a part of her identity.) Chabon began, in his fiction and in an ever-increasing portfolio of engaging and intimate personal essays, to measure the impact of both his religion and his family on his fictional sensibility. "I wanted to know where I came from, to retrace my steps and see if I dropped anything along the way that might serve me, now, better than I had imagined at the time of letting it go" (*Maps and Legends* 190). All the while, he maintained a cutting-edge website, one of the first writers of serious fiction to do so, through which he communicated with a growing nation of fans/readers—he actually listed his email address in the author information on the jacket flap of *Wonder Boys*—all the while entertaining them with off-the-cuff observations and irreverent postings that recalled his own adolescent love of *MAD* magazine and Monty Python.

Although now confident in his talent, Chabon was nevertheless restless. In an otherwise appreciative review of *Wonder Boys, Washington Post* book critic Jonathan Yardley famously challenged the young novelist to attempt something a bit grander and more daring than essentially first-person explorations of well-heeled, well-educated characters playing out their quests for identity while happily lodged within the comfortable insulation of academia. The implication was clear: Chabon needed to tackle the scale and scope of a larger project or risk being labeled a lightweight. He took the challenge to heart. In one of those serendipitous moments, Chabon was paging through a *Smithsonian* magazine when he chanced upon a feature on Jerry Siegel and Joel Shuster, the creators of Superman, and more generally on 1940s Manhattan and the Golden Era of American comics. It brought back memories of his own childhood infatuation with D.C. and Marvel comics. (When he was fifteen, he had sold off most of his massive collection to testify to his own maturity and now had only a single box of them.) Rereading them now, marveling over their intricate artwork and wonderfully bizarre plot lines, Chabon retapped his deep love of this distinctly American pop-culture medium and began what would prove to be a massive research investigation into comic books themselves, their Golden Era just before the Second World War, and New York City between the world wars, the epicenter of the burgeoning industry. He threw himself into the project and immersed himself in the narrative architecture of classic comic books; he walked the streets of Brooklyn to absorb their ambience; he interviewed surviving comic-book wunderkinds from the 1940s; he listened devotedly to Big Band swing; he meticulously studied dozens of period histories, cultural studies, political works, as well as technical manuals on animation and graphic design. And for the first time, Chabon was prepared to position his faith as a central element of his fiction—the comic book creators he began to imagine into characters would both be Jewish, as were most of the comic book pioneers.

Still smarting from the difficult experience of "Fountain City" but now buttressed by the support of his wife and family, Chabon found in the four years of this project a new confidence, the multiple plotlines, the burgeoning cast of characters, and the nearly forty years of narrative action cohering into a satisfying design. Although the manuscript was remarkably more developed than his previous fiction, Chabon used the comic book genre to explore a familiar theme: the role of the imagination, here tested amid an unforgiving twentieth century, represented specifically by the Nazi terrorism against European Jews. In Depression-era Brooklyn, two young Jewish cousins—one a practicing magician and gifted illustrator who smuggles himself out of Hitler's Czechoslovakia in a coffin, the other, a warehouse clerk who dreams of being a novelist and who can effortlessly concoct the most fantastic story lines—invent a surprisingly successful comic-book superhero, the masked, stern-jawed Escapist. Issue to issue he single-handedly defeats the insidious agents of evil stalking the European continent even as Hitler and his cohorts grow menacingly virulent.

The work, *The Amazing Adventures of Kavalier & Clay,* appeared in 2000. Critical response greeted the work as a major publishing event, touting it as a narrative tour de force and linking its confident deployment of historical fact and enthralling fiction, its polished and dense prose line, and its audacious scale to other landmark contemporary works. These included *Underworld,* Don DeLillo's massive cultural biography of the Cold War; *Mason & Dixon,* Thomas Pynchon's ambitious retelling of the late eighteenth-century surveying expedition; *Cloudsplitter,* Russell Banks's faux-memoir of the son of radical abolitionist John Brown; and *American Pastoral,* Philip Roth's impassioned look at the impact of the counterculture in the 1960s and 1970s. Although somewhat discomfited once again by Chabon's determined movement toward a happy ending and by the odd notion of such rich nostalgia for the 1930s being voiced by a writer born in 1963, critical opinion catapulted the book into national prominence and once again onto best-seller lists. (The faux-nostalgia was sustained as much by Chabon's ingestion of an impressive amount of research, documented by the book's hefty bibliography, as by long talks with his father, to whom Chabon dedicated the book, who had happily shared animated recollections of his childhood in Brooklyn during the era). *Kavalier & Clay* was short-listed for both the National Book Critics Circle Award and the prestigious PEN/Faulkner Award and was awarded the 2001 Pulitzer Prize for Fiction. It was optioned—although never produced—as a major motion picture project.

Not yet forty, but with three critically acclaimed best-sellers and the Pulitzer to his credit, and poised to become a fixture in any informed discussion of American post-Pynchon fiction, Chabon deliberately set about reinventing himself over the next decade in a most remarkable, indeed singular, evolution. He was not content to revisit the kind of story that had become his signature: realistic narratives of introspective, creative, nerdy isolates, gifted/cursed with energetic imaginations who come at last to tap (or in some cases to rue) the tonic wonder of community and the tectonic impact of love. After *Kavalier & Clay,* Chabon's fictional sensibility would take a most intriguing turn. It is of course tempting to speculate on the dramatic evolution. Perhaps because, in the course of producing the landmark *Kavalier & Clay,* Chabon had rediscovered in comic books his unironic adolescent infatuation with unaffected storytelling; perhaps because, as his own family evolved, his children had allowed him to recover the uncomplicated enchantment of stories unencumbered by the decidedly adult expectations of gravitas; perhaps because, reaching midlife, he was determined to test the range and reach of his narrative skill set, restless within any premature pigeonholing of his work as historical realism or psychological realism; or perhaps in the difficult aftermath of the national trauma of the September 11th terrorist attacks, he was seeking to affirm the abiding faith, part of his rediscovery of his Jewish identity, in the ancient consolation of storytelling as a way to minister to a culture in shock, a people in a dark time who needed the safe house, even temporarily, of story.

Whatever the motivation, across the first decade of the new millennium, Chabon upended the expectations of both his reader-nation and the critical establishment that had both come to expect—and to anticipate—his elegant realism and his vivid, sympathetic characters. Chabon embarked on a robust, decade-long investigation into the reach and scope of the imagination by testing, with brio and confidence, a wide-range of hoary genres that had long been dismissed by establishment critics as low-octane market-driven entertainments. Few contemporary writers of serious fiction who had achieved Chabon's level of success would have so deliberately and so completely abandoned their template narrative. Over the new millennium's first decade, Chabon maintained a most prodigious, if eccentric, output. He completed a sprawling young-adult fantasy epic-qua-sports novel set in four alternate worlds (*Summerland*); an intricate World War II detective story featuring an octogenarian Sherlock Holmes (*The Final Solution*); a stylish genre-busting detective noir murder mystery/political thriller/alternate history sci-fi hybrid (*The Yiddish Policemen's Union*); and a swashbuckling adventure tale in the manner of Dumas, set in Medieval Russia, about a usurped prince (*Gentlemen of the Road*). In addition, Chabon shepherded the publication of a series of comic-book projects through Dark Horse Comics based on superheroes and villains he had invented in *Kavalier & Clay*, and he even authored a series of grisly gothic horror stories under the pseudonym August Van Zorn, a fictional writer whose suicide deeply affects a young Grady Tripp in *Wonder Boys.*

Chabon also pursued a number of potentially lucrative film projects, as much for the money (as he candidly admitted) as for the chance to explore the dynamic between story and image, between character and setting, and between dialogue and visual argument that had intrigued him long ago when he had first read the comics books his grandfather had given him. Although many of the projects (some based on Chabon's own novels) ended up shelved or mired in studio politics, Chabon contributed significantly to the evolution of the script for 2004's critically-hailed *Spider-Man 2*. Add to that work the body of confessional essays published in print and online in which Chabon anatomized with honesty and bluntness his life as a writer, as a husband, and, perhaps most poignantly (given his own parents' divorce) as a father. What emerges is a most prolific decade in which Chabon stubbornly, joyously defied easy categorization. It was a decade in which Chabon confidently investigated narrative's privilege to entertain, producing a wide range of writings that reanimated genres long disdained by stiff-necked establishment elitists, predictably suspicious over the aesthetic value of anything with wide appeal. But Chabon vigorously defended the concept of serious fiction that nevertheless entertained, seeing within that dynamic a powerful magnetic pull between reader and writer all but lost over the last generation. Obscurantism had defined the heyday of postmodernism in which ambitious works of so-called serious fiction had routinely settled gently, undisturbed in the tomb dust of university libraries. Imagine, he argued, serious fiction that entertained, extending to his reader what had long been the privileged consolation of his own misfit characters: the temporary retreat into the entirely symbolic landscape of delightful fictions. "The original sense of the word 'entertainment' is a lovely one of mutual support through intertwining, like a pair of trees grown together, interwoven, each sustaining and bearing up the other. It suggests a kind of midair transfer of strength, contact across a void, like the tangling of cable and steel between two lonely bridgeheads. I can't think of a better approximation of the relation between reader and writer" (*Maps and Legends* 15).

Given Chabon's robust output and the manifest testimony of his imaginative vigor, and given the fact that he is still only in his early fifties with undoubtedly decades of productivity ahead, it is nevertheless tempting to see 2012's *Telegraph Avenue,* published after much delay to glowing reviews, as a kind of capstone text. Chabon returned to the rich energy of psychological realism, a reaffirmation, after a grand decade of sampling with hip-hop abandon a stunning range of eccentric genres that had taken him into increasingly fabulous realms, of what had first enthralled him and had gained his earliest readers: engaging, imaginative storytelling, a rich and complicated weave of plots and subplots; a cast of convincing multidimensional characters who animate a recognizable and very contemporary setting; the compassionate investigation into the complicated dynamic of love and marriage, work and friendship, sickness and mortality; the compelling momentum of urgent and entirely believable dilemmas; a cache of unobtrusive and richly suggestive symbols; syllable-crisp dialogue; gripping showdown scenes; a hip celebration of a wide range of pop culture (music, television, and film); and ultimately an ending that soars toward a complex optimism—all set to his signature prose line, at once lyric and muscular, ornate and relaxed.

Unlike his experiments over the previous decade, *Telegraph Avenue* takes place in a recognizable here and how. It is 2004 in Chabon's own neighborhoods of Berkeley. Two entrepreneurs—Archy Stallings, an African American jazz musician, and Nat Jaffe, a Jewish audiophile hopelessly enamored with vinyl—are determined to maintain their tiny, perpetually failing used-record shop (appropriately named Brokeland Records). They defend it against the threats posed by the imminent arrival of a much ballyhooed sprawling mega-music store a scant two blocks away and by the burgeoning downloading and pirating traffic on the Internet. That narrative, of course, plays an engaging variation on Chabon's career-long fascination with the solace of shelter against the encroachment of a hard reality: neither Archy nor Nat, despite being fortyish, are particularly interested in growing up, and both see their little shop as a kind of Neverland. Chabon deftly introduces three critical counter-narratives that further underscore that tension: one involving the two store-owners' wives, professional midwives, and their nasty legal entanglements against a hospital after a home delivery goes terribly wrong, a lawsuit that brings with it ugly suggestions of racism; another involving the return of Archy's errant father, a former martial-arts master turned movie star who had made a career in two underground classic B-movie blaxploitation films in the 1970s; and a third involving the return of Archy's own teenaged son, an emotionally damaged refugee from his first marriage who shows up unexpectedly from Texas and who quickly becomes entangled in a sexual relationship with Nat's teenaged son.

Of course *Telegraph Avenue* risks, as do all narratives so evidently informed and shaped by a writer's love of the sprawling family epics of the High Victorian Era, devolving into manipulative pathos and sentimental melodrama, the soapy stuff of nighttime cable dramas. (Chabon unsuccessfully pitched a loose version of the original story conception, a family drama based on the black and white dynamic that reflected the diversity of post-Reagan Berkeley, and even the title *Telegraph Avenue* as a pilot for a TNT series in the mid-1990s). Yet for veteran readers of Chabon, *Telegraph Avenue* continued Chabon's investigation into the tension between the heavy press of disappointment and loss and the sheltering solace of the imagination, between the difficult navigation of the emotional traumas of love and the perplexing fears and anxieties of family and the sweet slide into the easy clatter-wash of aesthetic retreats.

But *Telegraph Avenue* marked a major new direction for Chabon. With bold maturity, Chabon here challenges his own era to tap the rich energy of the imagination to transcend entrenched boundaries of race, gender, sexual orientation, and income. Consequently it is among the first—and most sweeping—narratives of the Obama era. The then-unknown Illinois state senator even appears in a cameo, when he comes to Berkeley to fire up a Kerry for President rally. Although a lifelong Democrat but never much of a political activist, Chabon was profoundly moved by Obama's 2008 barrier-transcending message of hope. (Ayelet and Obama were classmates at Harvard Law, and Chabon campaigned vigorously for the nominee.) In *Telegraph Avenue* then, Chabon trumpeted the imagination as a kind of mediating force that could bring a culture together, a far more potent conception of the imagination than, as it had long been for Chabon, consolation for socially awkward misfits uncertain about the vicissitudes of the real world.

With the bold Whitmanesque brio and robust reach of *Telegraph Avenue*, he had apparently come a long way from the nerdy kid with the flashlight poring over the Disney World map alone in his bedroom. But perhaps not so far. In June, 2011, with much fanfare and Internet buzz, actor-turned-film director Jon Favreau (*Elf, Iron Man, Cowboys & Aliens*) announced plans to devote his considerable creative energies to directing a blockbuster Disney summer film project scheduled for 2014. The high-concept, real-life/CGI-animated adventure film would bring together the live-action cinema savvy of Disney Studios and the cutting-edge animation technologies of Pixar. The film, entitled *Magic Kingdom,* would be set in Disneyland's Magic Kingdom theme park. There for a getaway, a family would become entangled in an alternate world that links the park's famous attractions, the rides, and their familiar personages coming to life as the family must navigate their way back to the real world, an adventure that would be as exhilarating as it would be harrowing. Although details about the plot were naturally kept quiet,

Favreau announced at the time that Pulitzer Prize–winning writer Michael Chabon had joined the project as lead scriptwriter. Disney had used Chabon before to tweak scripts for *Tron: Legacy,* the martial arts fairy tale *Snow and the Seven,* and the fantasy adventure epic *John Carter*. None of them, however, had sparked Disney magic at the box office.

Naturally, given the vagaries of Hollywood productions, the *Magic Kingdom* film project may never see completion. But few writers would be better tuned to such a project than Chabon, the kid who had survived the onset of the furious tempest of his parents' divorce by imagining his way into a secret kingdom beneath Disney's enchanted world. As it turns out, that desperate and vulnerable kid had tapped into what would become for the adult Chabon a most tender obsession: the shelter of the imagination and the difficult navigation into its welcoming environs and the tricky extrications out of its claustrophobic enclosures. In characters from Art Bechstein to Archy Stallings, from young Nathan Shapiro to the curmudgeonly Meyer Landsman, Chabon chronicles the troubled crossing-over into adulthood, the perplexing implosion of a family, the ignorance of homophobia or anti-Semitism or racism, the crass demands of career and the marketplace, or the hard reality of death. He affirms the vitality and vigor of the imagination in a hi-tech world that has all but lost touch with its consolation and its energy, offering the imagination initially as shelter. The safety it affords is a welcome respite from the complexities of a world that stubbornly refuses to be what we can so easily imagine it might be, and it ultimately serves as potent catalyst for genuine social and cultural change.

CHAPTER 2

The Mysteries of Pittsburgh

In a passing (if revealing) moment, Art Bechstein, the narrator of Chabon's debut novel, a recent University of Pittsburgh graduate and son of a Baltimore gangster, finishes a cigarette outside the university library. He pauses to gaze down, serenely, on the working-class neighborhoods that border the university, dreary rundown environs that stretch beneath him like some carefully scaled model world, "kids playing tiny baseball, the distant figures of dogs snatching at a little passing car, a miniature housewife on her back porch shaking out a snippet of red rug." Disconnected from such reality, Art positions himself far above its self-evident tackiness. In a jolting epiphany that pleases Art as much as it discomforts the reader, Art determines "to never become that small, and to devote [him]self to getting bigger and bigger and bigger." Far from the braggadocio of a college graduate poised now to tackle the world, he professes it more as a "sudden, frightened vow."[1] The moment reveals early on a strategy of desperate retreat by a man-child. He will ultimately renounce rather than engage the risks and joys, pains and rewards of ordinary life and use the elaborate dodge of a first-person confession to nimbly elude revelation and later to skip free altogether of the heavy burden of genuine intimacy. *The Mysteries of Pittsburgh* is a deceptively simple narrative that recalls a classic American novel Chabon later acknowledged as his template. Looking back at the origins of his first novel nearly a quarter of a century after its publication, Chabon recalled just beginning graduate studies at the University of California at Irvine, pacing about his under-furnished basement apartment and wrestling with the inchoate urgency to begin writing a Big Novel. His eyes happened to light on his well-thumbed copy of F. Scott Fitzgerald's *The Great Gatsby.* "I lay on the bed, opened its cracked paper covers . . . and this time *The Great Gatsby* read *me*. . . . [It] did what every necessary piece of fiction does as you pass through the fruitful phase of your writing life: it made me want to do something just like it" (*Maps and Legends* 151). Like Fitzgerald, Chabon uses a mesmerizing shadow-show narrative—a highly charged emotional drama involving both doomed love and violent death—as a fetching distraction from his far more subtle concern: a formal investigation into the dynamics of narrative itself. He specifically employs a first-person narrator to interrogate the very premise of narration: how a story in the hands of a naïve, and terrified, romantic becomes the central story.

Although *The Mysteries of Pittsburgh* is not simply a transposition of *The Great Gatsby* into a contemporary key, it is rewarding to approach it for what Chabon has told us it is: an hômage to Fitzgerald's classic anatomy of a hungry heart, hungry (and Art Bechstein is always ravenous, always on his way to or from a big meal) for something beyond the tawdry cycle of lust and dust, the world just as it is. The ties between the two narrators are fascinating. Like Nick Carraway, Art Bechstein faces a threshold summer—Nick is turning 30, Art is graduating college—and both are quietly anxious, poised on the tedium of what they perceive as a long stretch of ordinary life. Like Nick, Art is strikingly alone despite the furious social busyness about him. He lacks a significant love interest and is a loser with women who has long avoided the possibility of his own homosexuality. Like Nick, Art is an unabashed romantic (witness his cloying penchant for crying with little provocation often at the discomfort of companions), a man-child whose tender heart is unavailable to irony, who possesses a sense of easy exaggeration and seductive wonder appropriate to a child. (Indeed Art has matured little from the boy who was certain that the ocean was fruit juice.) Like Nick, Art is a devout narcissist who compulsively flattens everyone he meets into convenient and manageable stereotypes that, in turn, suspend any responsibility to engage others' depths as when he acknowledges his "ugly fondness for generalities" (*The Mysteries of Pittsburgh* 96). Like Nick, Art has lived by not living (he fancies himself to be like a wall), a riskless non-life spent observing rather than engaging, imagining life that goes on in homes that he visits and behind the bay windows he passes. "I had always felt pleasure on looking into the houses of strangers. . . . to be confronted by the simple, wondrous fact of other kitchens, other clocks, and ottomans" (191).

As a narrator, like Nick, Art self-consciously fashions gorgeous sentences that are at once elegant and purplish, tonic prose that begs to be read aloud and savored. Like Nick, Art inhabits a social environment that cannot sustain clear edges, one that is so rife with alcohol (and, in Art's case, recreational pharmaceuticals) that it makes inevitable a blurred sense of reality and in turn makes for too-frequent moments of perfect "drunken perception" (22). Like Nick, Art is determined to coax from the tawdry stuff of that immediate world the convincing animé of high drama, a Midas-styled strategy in which everything he touches he turns to the fine gold of his perception. This is a desperate strategy to avoid that necessary settling into the real world that marks the traditional maturation into adulthood. And in the end, like Nick, Art is finally overwhelmed by the realities of that complicated world and opts for voluntary exile (Nick back to the Midwest, Art to Europe), a hopeless plan to preserve the integrity of his romantic vision. And as with Fitzgerald's narrative, we are invited to buy into this vision: like Nick, Art's lyric voice is seductive. But as with *The Great Gatsby,* such complicity comes only at profound peril, the abdication of the reader's own clear-sightedness. Art's elaborate confessional narrative is as gorgeous as it is flimsy. We recall Art's fascination with the decrepit factory that borders the university. With the easy wonder of a child, he pretends that the factory's blackened brick chimney belches out the near-perfect clouds that float over the city. In turn Art similarly manufactures that airiest of illusions: the beautifully rendered story he tells.

Although acknowledging the bildungsroman genre as the cliché exercise of too many first-time novelists, critical response to the work hailed Chabon's adept plotting and his confident prose line. He was unlike the so-called nihilistic Brat Pack (East Coast New Wave fiction writers close to Chabon's age, most notably Bret Easton Ellis and Jay McInerney) or the academically fashionable minimalists (most prominently Raymond Carver), all of whom drew their stylistic model from Hemingway's stripped-down prose. Instead Chabon recalling a latter-day John Updike or John Cheever indulged a high-caloric love of language, his sentences deftly terraced, the merest observations stylishly ornamented with elaborate metaphors and exotic vocabulary. As with the heroes of all bildungsromans, Art Bechstein struggles with who he is, specifically over questions about his family and more profoundly about his sexual identity. He is conflicted about his father and his entrenched ties to the Baltimore mob and about the mysterious death years earlier of his beloved mother, a quiet woman whom he remembers played piano "like an angel" (179). And his am-I-am-I-not conflict over his sexual identity (at one point he even flips a coin to decide which lifestyle he will pursue) centers over two affairs he conducts simultaneously during the narrative present, the languid summer after his graduation: one a conventional romance with a seductive French literature major; the other, one far more fraught with unsettling implications, with a gay twenty-five-year-old undergraduate library intern.

At first approach, then, much about *The Mysteries of Pittsburgh* would appear to promise head-on engagement, a thinly veiled autobiographical first novel, another bildungsroman from yet another fledgling MFA., according to the prime directive of the most pedestrian undergraduate writing seminar, limited to the available materials of his own experience. After all, the character of Art Bechstein (rendered in the immediacy of first-person) shares much with its creator: both are good-looking, affluent, Jewish; both are Maryland natives; both are recent University of Pittsburgh graduates; both are on the difficult threshold of adulthood; both struggle with a problematic father and a fractured family; and both test the possibility of their own bisexuality. And given the first-person voice, we expect honest accounting—after all Art is completing a degree in the exacting ledger-science of economics. But like Fitzgerald's narrator, a Prufrockian bond salesman, Art Bechstein (who toils joylessly as a clerk in a soul-smothering off-campus chain bookstore with crass, supermarket-styled fluorescent lights) reveals himself to be too enamored, too carried away if you will, with the elaborate simplifications of his own imagination and a bit too comfortable with its implicit strategy of retreat. It is Art Bechstein, not Chabon, who drives the narrative—as he tells us in passing, he lives in the old chauffeur's quarters of a rambling genteel mansion once home to Pittsburgh's wealthy. Thus, despite the inclination to sympathize with any first-person narrator so apparently intent on revelation, we must be careful. Chabon cautions that we are in the hands of a manifestly unreliable narrator, a character who freely endorses wildly extravagant retreats from fact. In one scene, he gets all sentimental and sloppy when he hears Patti Page's "Old Cape Cod" on the radio, feeling unearned nostalgia for a song released before he was born and celebrating a quaint unspoiled beach that he had never visited. In fact Art grows little in his narrative. In the opening, when his father asks about his plans for the summer, Art admits to wanting to ascend the elevator of a fabulous thousand-story hotel and board a magnificent zeppelin tethered to that building's top-most mooring and then happily drift away. Later in the closing paragraph, after a summer of tumultuous experiences, Art cautions us that any confession, any recollection of his threshold summer, is most likely a distortion, an elegant exaggeration.[2]

Thus, Chabon's first novel works as a sort of anti-bildungsroman, a radical primer in the energy of the imagination, the novel's much-admired luxuriant prose line symptomatic less of Chabon's style and more of his character's enchantment with the spell of words and the astonishing power of the imperial self to create (and then inhabit) sturdy symbolic constructs, Oz-worlds where hard reality is blurred into cozy mystery. Book-fed and image-fat, Art effortlessly sees the real world as a collision-collage of high-culture and low-culture referents. He mentions, among others, Joan Crawford, Mamie Van Doren, Jennifer Jones, Bruce Springsteen, Nancy Drew, *The Wizard of Oz, Duck Soup,* Jackie Wilson, Charlton Heston, Jane Austen, Stevie Wonder, the Marx Brothers, Godzilla, Coleridge's opium-induced fragment "Kubla Khan" and Dr. Seuss, revealing a life spent interred in a symbolic world of artifacts. In evacuating to the romantic exoticism of Europe, Art happily withdraws into a safe-house world far from the pressing realities of dreary Pittsburgh. Far from resolving the mysteries of Pittsburgh, Art in the end demands them. Clarity is anathema for Art. Indeed his narrative begins literally with the departure of clarity: in the opening paragraph, he tells us that he has just broken up with his girlfriend of two years, the aptly named Claire, who has taken her Joni Mitchell records (with their stark confessional realism) and her soundtrack recording of Zeffirelli's *Romeo and Juliet* (with its sobering deflation of romantic love).

Thus much as with *The Great Gatsby,* we must begin by carefully assessing a problematic narrator. Art Bechstein has struggled heroically against facticity since the centering upheavals of his adolescence: first his mother's suspicious death when he was twelve (he was told she was killed in an auto accident, but any newspaper on the day of her death had mysteriously vanished from his home); and then six months later, his father's revelation, at Art's bar mitzvah, of underworld life as a gangster, Joe the Egg (a naïve Art had long thought his father a professional golfer and amateur painter). Reeling from the cataclysmic effect of such intrusive realities, Art had since insulated himself: he never speaks of his mother's death and even now when he meets his father for their occasional awkward luncheons the subject of the mob is never brought up. He terms it his family's "vague business," as if his family's considerable wealth had magically accumulated and the gun-toting, shadowy wise guys who come to their restaurant table are just run-of-the-mill business associates (9). Even now despite being a college graduate, Art appears, in his father's assessment, "doomed to terminal adolescence" (11). He willingly and happily lives in a comic-book world where everyone he meets maintains a secret identity. This tantalizing promise of fantastic revelation renders ironic and ultimately irrelevant the world as it is. Art can elegantly sidestep every difficult reality—he has even refashioned his persistent suspicions that he might be gay as garden-variety adolescent awkwardness, a long-term "crisis of self-esteem" (40).

Such strategic disconnection has come with a price. When brought too close to complicated realities, Art panics. When his father briefly reminiscences during a lunch about how beautiful Art's mother had been, Art brusquely excuses himself and hurries to the men's room where he vomits for "two hundred and forty thundering clicks of [his] quartz watch" (179–180). Art is afraid to live. His narrative begins right after his graduation, a traditional mark of commencement that here has been (predictably) delayed. Art happily lingers in the protective walls of the ivory tower toiling to complete one final pointless term paper, this one on Wilhelm Fliess, a confidant of Sigmund Freud, who (ironically given Art's own self-doubts) pioneered psychoanalytical theories on bisexuality. Facing imminent exile from the protectorate of the ivory tower, Art acknowledges a life spent apart, fascinated (even content) by observation and defined by a refusal to risk. Far from being discontented over such self-imposed isolation, Art disdains the logic of engagement and sees a threat in being simply ordinary. His worst nightmare is a recurring dream of "visiting an empty place where nothing happened with awful slowness" (42). Boredom, the settling into settling-in, the surrender to the smallness of the day-to-day, terrifies Art.

Rejecting the enticements of experience, fearing the consequences of entanglements, relishing the voyeuristic thrill of observing people (he likes stepping into rooms of strange houses and conjuring the lives of its occupants), Art is ready, he says with unconvincing brio in the opening pages, to change, to have a significant summer, ready now to live. He chances to meet that very evening, just outside the library, the intriguing Arthur Lecomte, a student, a professional house-sitter who works in the library (ironically in Acquisitions) and who, after the briefest snatch of casual chat, impulsively invites Art to a party. After a moment of contentious internal debate, Art agrees; it was time, he tells us, to live, "to land . . . in novel and incomprehensible situations" (17). Within a flurry of minutes, Art is climbing into a Fiat surrounded by strangers, all Arthur's friends, and is hurtling down Pittsburgh's congested main drag, heading to a party, although he does not know where, literally going along for the ride, swept up in the adrenaline rush of forced spontaneity under the charm of the alluring stranger.

As in the relationship between the gangster Jimmy Gatz and Nick Carraway, Arthur Lecomte, with his eccentric talent for origami, will entirely remake Art's sensibility much as he does the discarded cigarette cartons that he so deftly folds into surprising—if mysterious—shapes. (Art is never sure whether they are dogs or musical instruments.) Consider Art's over-the-top astonishment over a man he has just met: "[Arthur] had an effortless genius for manners; remarkable, perhaps, just because it was unique among people his age. It seemed . . . that Arthur, with his old, strange courtliness, would triumph over any scene he chose to make; that in a world made miserable by frankness, his handsome condescension, his elitism, and his perfect lack of candor were fatal gifts, and I wanted to serve in his corps and to be socially graceful" (31). Much as Gatsby does for Nick, Arthur will guide Art through galvanizing life experiences during the dizzying rush of a single summer—a tonic romance with a French literature major named Phlox Lombardi; a raucous (and doomed) friendship with a boyhood friend, Cleveland Arning; and ultimately a heady affair with Arthur himself. As narrator revisiting that summer, Art (as his name implies) will artfully reconfigure each one into simple, convincing cartoon-figures appropriate to his comic-book sensibility.

Consider the intoxicating Phlox Lombardi. While waiting for the elevator in the library the June evening that opens the narrative, Art notices an "odd, fragile girl" wearing aqua hair ribbons, sitting in one of the library's window ledges—but, of course, had done nothing about it despite the woman's lingering look at him (9). As it turns out, Arthur knows the girl. He introduces Art to her. Predictably, within Art's reconstructed narrative long after the fact, we get a deftly staged Hollywood-style cute meet. Even before she speaks, Art is captivated, a moment complete with a string-heavy "rush of Borodin" (47). The subsequent steamy affair with Phlox swiftly moves toward conventional questions of love and commitment. Stunningly attractive with her 1940s-style boy bangs and her deep-blue eyes, Phlox offers Art unexamined devotion and full-tilt sexual exercise (after all, she is a French Lit major). Despite her fascination with fetishistic sexual behavior, which she reveals to a stunned Art later in the summer, she abhors even the notion of homosexuality. After Art confesses his relationship with Arthur, Phlox breaks up via a lengthy tirade-letter in which she condemns homosexuality as repugnant. Later, however, she magnanimously "forgives" what she sees as Art's lapse. She then lures him to the library by having a friend who works there call Art claiming that a search and recovery process for a lost book charged to him could only be initiated by Art's coming personally to the library. Once Art is there, Phlox conducts a predictable seduction—her own search and recovery as it were—in an isolated study room to convince Art to come back to her and, by extension, to the evident rewards of heterosexuality. The seduction is hardly Hollywood tectonic—she presses him to declare his love with cloying persistence; unzips his pants like a child unwrapping a doll; describes Art's half-hearted erection as "handsome" and "polite"; hoists herself onto a study table, exposing her lack of panties ("Were you prepared for this?" asks a naïve Art); and then must encourage Art who dutifully sinks into her like a "hot bath" (258). The entire interlude takes just under a minute.

Of course Art is not so easily converted to heterosexuality. The reunion with Phlox ends disastrously after the library encounter when Phlox invites Art to her apartment. After their initial perfunctory consummation—loud and fast with Phlox entirely in control, Art "crouching on [his] elbows and knees"—Art clumsily requests anal intercourse (264). After terribly unromantic slathers of "cold petroleum jelly," Art loses heart when he attempts to enter the "pinched, plain orifice" (265). It fails of its own irony. The complex reality of his bisexuality presses too closely. As he edges precipitously toward those fundamental questions of who and what he is, Art does what Art does best: he sneaks out. While walking home under the appropriately fabulous starry night sky, Art wishes that he could just fly away to Mexico and "live irresponsibly in a little pink hotel" or to Italy to "sleep through blinding afternoons in a half-fallen villa" or simply vanish "into the railroad wastes of North America" befriending prostitutes and bartenders (265–266). The fantasies are at once fabulous and meticulously detailed—and, of course, as Chabon knows, unsettlingly childish. Rather than confront the complicated reality of his uncertain sexuality, Art simply, cleanly dreams of elaborate flight.

Chabon—and the reader for that matter—are far more intrigued by Phlox. To borrow the Fitzgerald template, Phlox Lombardi serves as the narrative's Daisy Buchanan, suggested not only by their floral names but also by their contradictory character. Who is Phlox Lombardi? Everything about Phlox (as with Daisy) tantalizes the reader—she remains to us a perplexing, maddeningly contradictory paradox that Art is too quick to simplify and ultimately reject, unprepared for the sheer complexity of her unnerving reality. Indeed before Art even meets the woman with blue ribbons who had caught his eye in the library, Arthur cautions him that she is erratic, volatile. Later Phlox admits to going through phases: after her born-again Christian phase (her favorite book is still Oscar Wilde's Christ-parable *The Selfish Giant*), she had done the "punk thing, the biker's girl thing, the seamstress thing, the prep school thing, and sort of the housewife thing, although [she] wasn't married" (100). During her undergraduate career, Phlox has used college (understandably) to test possibilities as part of that necessary journey toward identity, the evolution into complexity that marks the traditional emergence into selfhood. But Art has no vocabulary for that complexity and he struggles with such paradox. When he first meets Phlox, he is told her nickname is the fearsome sounding Mau Mau and that she is an angry punk, an assessment at odds with the quiet library-angel with blue ribbons in her hair whom Art had first noticed. But that appearance of gentility is decidedly at odds with Phlox's bold sexual adventurism (conducted in a number of public venues) and certainly with her prurient fascination with the literature of sadomasochism—on the same sticky June night she first tells Art that she loves him, she reads aloud to him on the front stoop of her apartment from the notorious *Story of O.* Although he recalls reading the book when he was thirteen (he found it among his mother's books just after she died—an interesting aside, the implications of which, typically, Art elects not to pursue), now he is "shocked to discover what an evil book it was, although nicely written, and the thought that it was [Phlox's] favorite" disturbs him (110).

Of course readers are better prepared than Art. We notice a poster of Greta Garbo in Phlox's apartment and on her end table a copy of Norman Mailer's book on Marilyn Monroe, all three iconic figures, consummate mysteries too-quickly flattened into accessible caricatures by thin-souled media types. Like the Twister floor game that Phlox impulsively has Art buy and then play, a game that combines the playful and erotic in contortions that are as much athletic as they are clumsy, Phlox embodies the mystery of paradox. She refuses to be simply anything. Like the heady perfume she wears—Opium—Phlox is as much enticing as she is addictive, as tectonic as she is destructive. She is kept at an intriguing distance from us. Art flattens Phlox into a conventionally shallow, even conniving femme fatale looking for a conventionally constricting relationship, but Phlox emerges with more nuance to the reader. Like Daisy (and like Marilyn and Garbo for that matter), Phlox is a vital, free-wheeling element, the novel's central mystery, a parallel to the Jennifer Jones character in the film *Portrait of Jennie,* which Phlox coos is her favorite movie. Phlox is the novel's living contradiction: a punk romantic, a sensual virgin, an accommodating bitch, an erotic Puritan, a frigid whore, a calculating free-spirit, a Machiavellian victim, a knowing fool, a selfish lover, a quixotic realist, a practical bohemian, a heartless saint, an idealistic materialist, an open-minded conservative, an honest liar, a sophisticated naïf, a flaky pragmatist. Chabon uses the mysterious figure of Phlox to expose his narrator's uneasiness over mystery, his preference for Crayola simplifications and, if confronted, for easy escape.

Art maintains a similarly distorted vision when he introduces into his summer narrative Arthur's boyhood friend, Cleveland Arning. For Art, Cleveland too quickly comes to embody the raw energy of anarchy that his own life of buttoned-down conformity has never touched. A renegade Catholic with a quirky taste for the morbid tales of Edgar Allan Poe, a leather-jacketed punk riding a loud machine, Cleveland literally roars into Art's life—he pulls up on his enormous BMW motorcycle, jumps the curb, and shatters the monastic quiet of Art's bookstore. Cleveland is tattooed, gargantuan, perpetually drunk, irreverent, streetwise. We only learn much later the painful circumstances behind such theatrical bravado—a bitter and distant father long suppressing his homosexuality, an unhappy mother driven, finally, to suicide. But within Art's narrow perspective, Cleveland represents simple, untutored spontaneity, the pulsing animation of which Art frequently terms with typical simplification as pure evil. He is the embodiment of the messy bohemian lifestyle that Art, despite his father's mob connection, has neatly skirted. While Art obscures his ties to organized crime, Cleveland flaunts it. He loudly identifies Art as a gangster's son when he first pulls up to the bookstore and makes no secret of his own association with low-level Pittsburgh mobsters. Indeed Cleveland plots ambitious strategies for career advancement within the syndicate and baldly declares that he wants to be big in the mob. Cleveland's job, collecting the exorbitant interest on illegal loans for local mobsters, prompts him to befriend Art: with calculated cool, he wants an introduction to Joe the Egg to launch his mob career. Art resists accommodating Cleveland. But Art accompanies Cleveland on a routine collection route and sees firsthand how his father's business operates. We see the sordidness of the syndicate's usury business and its real threats of violence against those pathetic desperates caught up in economic straits. But Art finds the house-to-house drama of collecting from those struggling to pay back the exorbitant loans enthralling theater, "terribly fascinating work" (191). The economics major does not recognize the troubling implications of these meager lives so perilously close to economic ruin and compelled to deal for street loans.

To us, of course, little about Cleveland Arning is grand save his own preposterous bloviating. He is a sorry cliché of a Beat sensibility that even by the time of the narrative, 1981, had already been thinned into parody. Art is fascinated by Cleveland's claim to be a writer, seeing in such a renegade lifestyle the redemptive savage grace of the nonconformist. The reputation, however, rests on a baseball novel Cleveland wrote when he was thirteen. His more recent writing is less grand: a twenty-thousand-word essay on cockroaches. We see a self-sustaining, self-justifying misfit with a huge gut and an ugly rattlesnake tie who has shot through all the money his father had left him, wasting it on dope, beer, and Grateful Dead tickets. Cleveland's voracious appetite for life is an unconvincing subterfuge played desperately against a dark private life of emotional tragedy, the depth of which Art sees but refuses to appreciate when he visits Cleveland's home. Rather than explore the dimensions of the actual traumas—a sexually conflicted father, a self-destructive mother, and a problematic relationship with a sister that Cleveland nearly blinded when, as a child, he threw rocks at her during a summer trip to Lake Erie—Art relishes a long night walk through the house (a thrill as if he were like a burglar) during which he simply imagines the "trouble, the tension" of the house (114). Although he was not present, Art even offers a stunningly detailed "memory" of the sister's near-blinding.

But it is Cleveland's sudden, violent death that signals to Art an end to his summer and ironically the need to avoid growing up and engaging the realities of his own life (typical of the bildungsroman). Instead he chooses to do what he does best: run. In the torrid last days of August, associates of Art's father hire Cleveland to rob affluent houses of jewelry that could, in turn, be fenced. He prepares for one of his night heists and imagines himself to be like the Grinch. Dressed in black, his heart thumping, he pauses in the shrubs of the swanky home to which he has been dispatched and momentarily watches the unsuspecting family as they gather for dinner. Carefully, taking measured swigs from a flask, he enters an unlocked ground floor window. He steps gingerly into a "cold, plutonian" (that is, Poe-like) library and makes his way to a "silent, black bedroom" to commence the burglary (275). But this theft goes terribly awry as the police unexpectedly show up just as Cleveland is exiting the home with the stolen jewelry stashed in a doll he had found. In the chaos of the ensuring chase, Cleveland on foot against both a squad of police cars and even a hovering helicopter, he desperately ascends to the catwalk of the Cloud Factory and there, in the hard glare from the crossing spotlights, he loses his footing and falls to his death. The narrative of Cleveland's final burglary is itself a most enthralling narrative, one of the novel's most riveting set pieces, richly detailed and meticulously re-created, until we realize that our narrator was not present for the burglary and only arrived in time to see Cleveland plunge to his death. What we are reading is pure confection. The most important words in nearly a dozen pages of gripping narrative are, as it turns out, the first two: "I imagine" (270). Art conjures a convincing enchantment that deftly refashions Cleveland's death into a bold, cinematic rendering of a burglary gone bad. As with Phlox, Art flattens a multilayered character—at once desperate and heroic, a mystery as impenetrable as the motorcycle face shield he sports—into caricature.

But no character engages Art's imagination more profoundly than the elegant Arthur Lecomte. Art is intoxicated by the exotic figure of Arthur Lecomte from the moment they meet outside the library in the gauzy light of that June twilight. Pink-skinned with golden stubble and gifted with a singularly gaudy sense of fashion, Arthur immediately enthralls Art with his caustic sarcasm, his devastating wit, his studied mannerisms, his hip literate allusions, and his wily dexterous conversation. He effortlessly coins Wildean aphorisms, embodying the haughty attitude of privilege and elite education. But Art taps a most profound hunger for Arthur. As with Nick Carraway, who needs the dimension of wonder embodied in his grand redesign of sleazy gangster Jimmy Gatz into The Great Gatsby, Art discovers in the elusive figure of Arthur Lecomte a figure commensurate to his capacity for wonder. The near-coincidence of their first names underscores how much Arthur reflects his creator. Gorgeously, effortlessly visual like Jimmy Gatz (Art meticulously records Arthur's outrageous wardrobe choices), Arthur Lecomte comes to the narrative a performance piece, a convincing collision of surfaces that the narrator readily gifts with depth and animation. As with Nick and Jimmy Gatz, we want to believe in the compelling gesture of The Great Lecomte: amid the gray, dreary press of the gritty working class environs of Pittsburgh, Arthur glitters. He is educated, hyper-cool, cultured, born to privilege and classic grace, animated by an unaffected wit, unforced charisma, and radiant charm. In addition Chabon introduces into his narrative what is at best an indirect element of the Fitzgerald work: the narrator's homoerotic impulse toward the subject of his imaginative reconstruction. There is no doubt about Art's erotic hunger for Arthur—he knows the moment they meet that Arthur is gay. Later in the sweltering summer heat by a posh country club pool, Art contemplates with rising lust the well-oiled, well-muscled figure of Arthur, inventorying with unseemly detail Arthur's legs, his stomach, his navel, his thighs, his chest, the pads of his muscles, the "fist" wrapped in his slick blue Lycra bathing suit. "I had never before given a man's body the regard I now gave his. . . . I felt, I feel, almost as if I did not have the vocabulary to describe it" (162). Weeks later they finally consummate (albeit clumsily)—Art finds it painful, the lubricating oil "cold and strange," but he does not want Arthur to stop (216). Art suffers a nosebleed, suggesting the loss of his gay virginity. If Art is uncertain over the implications of the act, Arthur surely is not. When they have finished, the triumphant Arthur waves the blood-stained pillowcase from his bedroom window.

But that seductive conjure, as with Nick's conjure of Jimmy Gatz, seldom brushes against reality. If the reader pulls back sufficiently, we see a different, more layered Arthur. We see Arthur's disdain for lesser people who fawn about him. We stare into his cold, blue eyes and see his Machiavellian willingness to use people for his own amusement. We feel the chill of his aloofness: like the reclusive Jimmy Gatz, Arthur describes himself as a free-floating atom, both a part and apart. We see his palpable arrogance, his chilling self-sufficiency. We see his calculating mercenary sensibility, his cultural shallowness, and his predatory need to exploit others. He is at best a poseur and a hypocrite and at worst a borderline sociopath. Despite caustically dismissing convention and flaunting his homosexuality and celebrating the bohemian nightlife, Arthur still attends daily Mass. His feral promiscuity, which never concerns Art, suggests a careless lifestyle, a flamboyant need for others to need him, a flip sense of the power of sexuality that borders on the parasitic. Indeed Art mentions without further comment that Arthur is undergoing treatment for scabies, a nasty skin rash (known as the seven-year itch) caused by burrowing parasites.

Much as Jimmy Gatz is no Great Gatsby, Arthur Lecomte is more complicated than what Art conjures. Arthur is actually both a sustained performance piece and just another unremarkable career undergraduate: over-read, over-impressed with his own charms, a lost soul at radical disconnect from his own roots, adrift in the drunken toss of rounds and rounds of parties. That he can be both intrigues us, but that he may be both does not even interest Art. At one point Art unexpectedly meets Arthur's mother late in July, long after he has fallen under Arthur's spell. She stops by unannounced at the off-campus residence her son is house-sitting to mend his worn shirts. The awkward moment recalls the scene in which Nick meets Jimmy Gatz's father, a North Dakota farmer. Art learns that Arthur was hardly born to privilege. In fact his mother still works cleaning houses, her devastated hands testifying to a life of long days of "submission to hard work and sorrow" (247). But the encounter does little to diminish the energy of Art's resilient conjure.

Art's simplification of Arthur shapes the narrative's closing. The story of Art's "momentous" summer is given a frame: Art has abandoned Pittsburgh for the protective sanctuary of a life overseas, an exile triggered, we are told, after Art watches Cleveland fall to his death. Art suspects his father might have arranged the ambush in fury over the details of Art's affair with Arthur, which is described in the letter from Phlox that Cleveland had stolen and (presumably) given to the father in a misguided attempt to gain the gangster's favor. But sitting in a hospital bed the day after Cleveland's death (amid the crowds and confusion surrounding Cleveland's dramatic plummet, Art is beaten by a police officer who mistakenly thinks he is resisting arrest), Art verges toward the moment when he must at last confront rather than avoid such complications. "I felt trapped, though I wasn't exactly certain of how; I no longer had a clear impression of where the alliances and fissures lay among the people I knew, of who stood on which side of me and in what relation; which was tantamount . . . to my forgetting who I was. For a moment . . . I was terrified, disconnected, falling" (288–289). It is a promising moment in a narrative in which the narrator had averted just such a potentially implosive encounter with reality. His mind galloping toward the unwanted epiphany of honest insight, Art begins to think of what he has long suppressed: the suspicion that his father's mob connections had had something to do with his mother's "accidental" death years ago, that perhaps that gentle, loving woman had been killed as some kind of warning to his father.

Art is moved to a position when questions critical to his maturity—Who am I? Who can I trust? Where can I turn?—press close, unanswerable questions that would reveal the paradoxical complexity at the heart of the human enterprise. When Art approaches the moment at which he will be gifted with a difficult awareness, as with countless narrators of other bildungsromans, the traditional mixed reward of maturity, he lays in a hospital bed, a common locale for such moments of therapeutic awareness. Add to that the heavy downpour from a thunderstorm outside as a potent image of baptism and rejuvenation, and Chabon prepares us for the traditional epiphany and the healing implications of clear sight. But at that very moment, Art Bechstein becomes instead the first in what will be a long line of Chabon's escape artists. Art elects to duck out. He never resolves questions about the death of his mother, the death of Cleveland, or his sexual identity, happily preferring the mysteries of Pittsburgh to remain exactly that. Told by a nurse that his father is waiting outside his door to see him, Art deftly dodges the meeting with her help. Early the next morning he gathers his scattered clothes, checks out of the hospital, and runs to Arthur. But Arthur has also experienced a blunt introduction to reality: muscle from the mob visits Arthur and strongly encourages him to leave town and specifically not to pursue any homosexual liaison with Art. Unlike Art, who is so completely inoculated against reality, the "ashen and sleepless" Arthur has every intention of heeding the advice (292). Art's solution is simple: run. At Art's insistence, they run together, ultimately heading to the openness of Europe. The outcome is not a complete success. We learn that Art is alone now in Barcelona—Arthur has left him and is living, Art thinks, in Majorca.

And from that safe haven, relaxed into the intoxicating charm of withdrawal, Art has written his confessional narrative, which he admits as he closes might be a grand and gaudy evasion, the manifestation of the centripetal energy of the imagination. Art declines to accept the mysteries of Pittsburgh: his bisexuality (in the narrative's frame, Art lingers lovingly over an old photo of Phlox but speaks as well of intimate café conversations with a young man, a lover we assume, who disdains women); his loving father who is a polished, educated, ruthless, predatory gangster; his lovers, Phlox and Arthur, who are at once deeply caring as well as manipulative control freaks capable of fathomless betrayals. Like Nick Carraway, he cannot sustain the courage necessary to survive within a paradoxical environment. He happily celebrates a resistance to clarity, rejects the gift of awareness, and ultimately avoids confrontations with those nagging, untidy questions about himself and his identity, questions that would naturally shape any man-child's evolution into maturity.

It is telling that the three works to which admiring critics most frequently compared *The Mysteries of Pittsburgh*—*Adventures of Huckleberry Finn*, *The Great Gatsby*, and *The Catcher in the Rye*—contain narrators who pathologically evade reality, freely indulge fantasies, and unapologetically lie, often without provocation, embellishing for the sheer delight of such extravagance. Like Fitzgerald, Twain, and Salinger, Chabon is not entirely convinced of the viability of the intoxicating lure of escape. As in *The Great Gatsby,* the narrator grows distant from the larger authority's endorsement. In effect, the narrator exemplifies what the author does not support. Chabon understands what his narrator rejects: retreat cannot persist, the evolution into maturity must be marked by a willingness to accept the wonder of mystery rather than the tidiness of certainty. Repeatedly exposed to the pressures of the real world—the itch of carnality, the predatory logic of betrayal, the tacky expectations of love, the emotional terrorism of family, the pressure of vulnerability and dependency, the grim reality of violence, the tawdriness of mercenary materialism, and above all the soul-starving routine of ordinary life—Art skillfully dodges them.

As in *The Wizard of Oz,* a fantasy narrative to which Art eludes, where the gaudy excess and splendid appointments of the Emerald City are sustained only by its citizens' voluntarily wearing emerald glasses, we are invited to don tinted glasses as it were and to surrender to the provocative simplifications of Art's imaginative vision. And in turn we must forgive him the romantic need for a cozy aura of mystery, his decision that flight and escape are finer strategies than honest confrontation, awareness, and clear sight. As suggested by the odd nickname Phlox gives him (Artichoke), in the end Art chokes. He cannot sustain the commitment to reality but rather invents (like Nick Carraway) a durable simulation, the narrative we are reading. When Art visits Phlox's off-campus apartment, he notices on her coffee table a remarkably lifelike porcelain statue of a white Persian cat. Phlox even fusses over the cat—she dotes on it, tickles its porcelain chin, and coos its name (Chloe) over and over to it in a baby voice. Phlox admits the statue is a stand-in—her landlord will not permit pets and her mother is currently taking care of the real Chloe. The stand-in, the model cat, is for her real enough, a simulation that will do because the real thing brings with it intolerable complications and inevitable (and painful) messiness.

So in the end Art slips free of messy reality and the dreary responsibility required of clear sight and awareness. Thus Chabon begins, as it were, in full retreat. There are surely worse offenses. Chabon offers a narrative teeming with unsavory lowlifes in the criminal underground to underscore the point. And to be honest, much as when we read Nick's revisioning of the feral gangster Jimmy Gatz, we are most reluctant to demand the traditional moment of twisting the narrative camera lens to clear. Art's narrative has a welcoming, enclosing feel, and we gratefully assent to his refusal to engage and even enjoy the projections. We relish Art's effortless way with language, much like those peaceful interludes Art spends mesmerized by the puffy confections of the Cloud Factory or later by the delicate soap bubbles Phlox so carefully animates. As readers we are not inclined (as would Nancy Drew, ironically one of Art's favorites) to dispel the mysteries of Art's life or to question his tacit offer to relax into his entirely symbolic landscape where such mysteries must never be confronted, where pivotal questions about identity need never be resolved. With the giddy zealousness of a first-time novelist, a freshly-minted M.F.A. just beginning to tap the power of language to conjure and relishing the sheer tensile strength of worlds constructed entirely of sentences and paragraphs, Chabon here entertains the most wonderful of what-ifs. *What if you could talk a private world into existence?* But Art Bechstein is only an opening gambit, one that Chabon will interrogate as, novel to novel, he tests the tension between the protective isolation of retreat and the hazardous implications of engagement, in short, the tension between the fabulous and the real.

CHAPTER 3

The Lost World Cycle

With the publication of *The Mysteries of Pittsburgh* when he was just twenty-four, Michael Chabon, enjoyed a most enviable position. His rookie novel garnered significant critical praise. It sold respectably and had even been optioned as a film project (although the film would not be completed for nearly a decade). And Chabon received unexpectedly generous attention at public readings and in interviews. His rock-star good looks and effortless charisma made him a kind of celebrity, a hot commodity, poised to become a major literary voice in the twenty-something generation. Indeed he even secured a lucrative advance against an as-yet-unstarted sophomore effort. Enthusiastically he cast about for a new project.[1] Strolling past a bookstore, he chanced to see in its display window a slender academic tome on post-modern art and architecture. Curious, he went in. And as he was paging through the volume, he came upon a contemporary watercolor painting of the original conceptual grid-layout of the nation's capital as conceived by the French architect Pierre L'Enfant.

Chabon was riveted by the intricate lines of an entirely invented city. Raised in a similarly prefabricated community and enthralled as a child by the controlled but playful environments of Disney's worlds, Chabon found himself there in the bookstore aisle oddly energized by the idea of laying out such a symmetric model world, like his younger self poring over the theme-park map of the Magic Kingdom. Over the next several weeks, he began outlining a novel, one more grandly conceived than his first, more ambitious and more daring, but one still very much centered on his fascination with the wide energy field of the imagination. As Chabon came to conceive it, the novel would focus on the relationship between an engagingly eccentric architect and his most reluctant apprentice-student, the son of a rabbi haunted by the suicide of a gay brother. The mentor-protégé relationship would allow Chabon to revisit the intricate dynamic between the doomed bohemian biker Cleveland Arning and the reserved economics major Art Bechstein.

But over months the project foundered. The manuscript grew exponentially, far beyond the reach of his largely untested authorial control. Recall Art Bechstein's dopey infatuation with the centripetal pull of the imagination and his adolescent eagerness to exile himself into a safe haven far away from the cutting mysteries of Pittsburgh, to construct a narrative, his own model world, where he could happily flatten characters into comic book two-dimensionality and effortlessly reduce emotional complexities into seductive simplifications and where the demanding work of engaging the difficult—and paradoxical—nature of the real need never intrude. Ironically, or perhaps fittingly, Chabon now became hopelessly entombed within a text-edifice of his own. Tentatively titled "Fountain City," the gargantuan manuscript ironically (or perhaps fittingly) described the visionary architect's mad dream of constructing a perfect baseball field in Florida near the gates of Disney's vast play-world, the template for Chabon's own adolescent infatuation with the energizing constructions of the boundless imagination. For more than five years, against the enormous pressure of the advance he had accepted and his increasing awareness of his diminishing celebrity, Chabon burned away within the cool friction of a manuscript that quickly grew into more than one thousand pages.

As with other fledgling writers who get caught within a Frankenstein novel-project that turns on its own creator, Chabon periodically broke free of the labyrinthine text to test the far friendlier confines of the short story. He found in its tailored demand for a clean beginning, tight middle, and clear end a bracing respite from a novel that was proliferating exponentially. Unlike that manuscript, in which Chabon furiously explored the reach of the full-throttle imagination, the short stories were far more modest. Indeed Chabon exposed his short-story characters to the measure and impact of the real world. They engaged rather than eluded facticity, struggled to adjust to the difficult mysteries of their worlds. Between 1987 and 1991, even as his frustrations mounted over the slow-motion crash and burn of his novel project, Chabon completed and published eleven stories in a variety of prominent magazines. Compared to *The Mysteries of Pittsburgh,* these stories, published collectively in 1992, were darker, more sobering. Gone is the breezy lightness of Art Bechstein and his twilight-magic summer, his elegant simplifications, his loony escapades, and his resilient determination to not to be bothered by the sobering consequences of growing up. Less like Fitzgerald and closer to John Updike or John Cheever, these were stories of grown-ups, stories of hard disappointment, bad luck, mercenary love, mismatched love, lost opportunities, festering grudges, the recklessness of carnality, casual dishonesties, petty violence, and utterly pointless death. These stories dismiss artists, dreamers, social misfits, and romantic innocents such as Art Bechstein as fools, blind and doomed. The epigraph to the collection, from poet Elizabeth Bishop, cautions as much: "More delicate than the historian's are the map makers' colors." If history—that is, story, narrative itself—is clumsy and inexact, Chabon would here test the clearer, cleaner colors of cartographers, those who, unlike historians, must stay far truer to the contours of the real.

In "S Angel," for instance, the story that opens the collection, Ira Wiseman (ironically known as I. Wiseman), a fourth-year drama student at UCLA, falls madly and hopelessly in love with a mysterious older woman with beatific gray eyes and luscious red lips. He chances to see her at the lavish wedding reception of his cousin, Sheila, a woman he had once dated. For her part, Sheila is oddly uninterested in celebrating her nuptials and barely looks at her new husband. When a bridesmaid happily brokers a dance between Ira and the mysterious woman, he is cautioned that the woman is nearly twice his age and on medication as part of her recovery from a messy divorce. But emboldened by tequila, Ira does not just want to dance with her—he wants to fall in love, wildly, recklessly because he "had never written villanelles or declarations veiled in careful metaphor, had never sold his blood plasma to buy champagne or jonquils, nor haunted a mailbox or a phone booth or a certain café."[2] All the elements are in place for a Hollywood-style romantic comedy. When the two dance they are wonderfully in sync. But the moment is rudely shattered when the woman, a hard-core real-estate agent, suddenly bolts from the reception to pursue a potentially lucrative deal. (The title comes from the phrase "Los Angeles" as it appears on the folded city map she carries to track her real-estate dealings.) She leaves Ira crestfallen and frustrated. But there is little time for self-pity. Ira is told that Sheila, angered over a guest ripping the train of her dress, has abruptly fled her own reception. When Ira finds her hiding in the hotel lobby, the two share a deeply ironic and very troubling kiss—a love that is as inexplicable and consequential as it is misdirected and pointless. Similarly, in the next story "Ocean Avenue," a chance encounter in a coffee shop between former partners gives them a chance to vent simmering resentments about the petty dimensions of the breakup of what was apparently a tempestuous relationship. The conversation quickly climaxes with the woman tossing a cup of hot espresso into the man's face and storming away. And like Ira, a desperate romantic, he chases her down the street and passionately, inexplicably, kisses her.

But that tone, quirky and quietly ironic, considerably darkens in "A Model World." Levine, a graduate student in meteorology studying the eccentric science of controlling clouds (nephokinesis), is determined to sabotage his own dissertation because he has begun to see it as a pointless endeavor. He longs to head to the mountains of New Mexico and craft ceramic wind chimes. In turn he deliberately plagiarizes, word for word, seven pages of an obscure paperback on clouds he happens to find among other forgotten books in a whiskey crate in a used bookstore, certain that he will not get away with it. The more he types passages from the forgotten book into his own dissertation, however, he comes to feel a kinship with its forgotten author. Suddenly eager to share his findings with his dissertation director, he (and his friend, a drama student named Smith who is having an affair with the dissertation director's wife, an actress) invite themselves over to the professor's house while he is having a get-together. After smoking a joint with the professor in his study, Levine is convinced in pot-induced paranoia that the obscure book is actually there on the professor's bookshelf.

Compelled to honesty, Levine blurts out not that he has plagiarized his dissertation but rather that Smith is sleeping with the professor's wife. The professor is nonplussed. When they return to the party, the guests decide to switch off the lights and play a kind of confess-all game—in the protective darkness, each guest would reveal the worst thing they have ever done. Smith goes first. Rather than admit he is cuckolding the host, however, he cops to a petty offense: as a kid, he spattered model airplane paint on a friend's new Matchbox car. In the closing paragraph, Smith reveals that he has gone on to success in his field (staging an original drama based on the life of Werner Heisenberg, appropriately the dark prophet of uncertainty) and that Levine has published his dissertation, with its plagiarized passages, to great acclaim, setting him up in a cushy tenure-track position.

In "Blumenthal on the Air," a Dallas-born disc jockey, now working late-night on a low-wattage jazz station in Paris, has married a gloomy and plain Iranian woman to help expedite her citizenship papers and realizes that he now loves her. But it is manifestly pointless. His futile attempts to hold even meager conversation with her are played out against her decision to leave him. Ironically she announces this amid the fireworks of Bastille Day, a celebration of the independence Blumenthal so desperately does not seek. In "Smoke," a second-rate pitcher five years beyond his prime struggles to reclaim his fastball even as coaches and journalists alike tell him it is gone for good. He heads to the chilling exile of Triple-A ball but only after he attends the funeral of a promising catcher cut down in his prime, killed in a car accident, extinguished like smoke.

Again and again in these stories, characters must surrender their fantasies to brutal fact; greed and mercenary self-interest trump romance; clear sight and honesty prove ironic; and romance leads only to soul-crushing disappointment. Reality offers little promise, little magic, and little wealth. Perhaps the signature moment in this collection occurs in "Millionaires," the last story before *The Lost World* cycle. It is spring and the daffodils are in bloom, a time for love. Vince, a late-night disc jockey in Pittsburgh, decides at last to act on his long infatuation with Kim, the stunning girlfriend of his best friend Harry, a toy designer, after the couple breaks up. Kim is a chain-smoking cocktail waitress at a local dive where she is known for enforcing order by wielding a baseball bat. (In the aftermath of their breakup, Harry sports an unexplained black eye). Although Harry begs Vince not to pursue Kim, the next day Vince is off to woo her, certain that Harry's warning reflects only petty jealousy. A hapless romantic, Vince feels he deserves at last to fall in love.

The conversation between the two, however, is awkward. After Vince tries clumsily to pull her into an embrace, Kim breaks free to ask Vince to do her a favor: return a large Seagram's box, taped shut and marked "Treasure," that Harry had left in her apartment. Vince opts to bury the box unopened in Kim's backyard, and then the two impulsively go to bed together. In the morning Kim tells Vince that she is carrying Harry's baby. Suddenly we understand that Harry, like Art Bechstein, prefers his game-world of toys and refuses such grown-up responsibility, his unborn child the real treasure he has abandoned. Years later, long after his marriage to Kim collapses of its own irony (it lasts only seven months) and long after Kim and her son have disappeared, Vince visits Harry. Untroubled by his long-ago decision to abandon his own child, Harry now shows Vince the prototype of his latest toy project: tacky cardboard doubloons, their paint dusted in flecks of real gold. Despite the patent evidence of their inauthenticity, even as the faux-gold luster literally comes off in his hands, Vince whispers, "We're rich." The irony of the statement underscores Chabon's larger, darker vision: little that glitters in the real world is golden.

With its stark deflation of the magic of love and its bleak sense of empty carnality and lost opportunities, "Millionaires" is in many ways a perfect segue into *The Lost World* cycle that closes the collection. Originally published in the *New Yorker* between 1987 and 1990, the ambitious cycle of five stories summarizes Chabon's sobering exploration of the vulnerability implicit in engaging the real world. The series spans six years that track young Nathan Shapiro's difficult emergence into adulthood and his struggles (like a young Chabon) to accept the implications of his parents' divorce and the subsequent reconfiguring of their lives with new lovers. The stories reveal how Nathan at least initially invests in desperate strategies of escape that surely recall Art Bechstein and the protective symbolic landscapes of make-believe. The nerdy Nathan is a bookworm who reads escapist exotica, mostly lurid science fiction and James Bond thrillers. He relishes long afternoons playing a fantasy baseball board game with his father. He lingers preternaturally within the mausoleum-cool refuge of branch libraries; he earnestly plays an interplanetary castaway in an elaborate neighborhood game with his friends. He dreams grandly of being a Medieval knight errant on a splendid charge, a comic-book superhero, and even the infant Moses poised on greatness. Nathan even hides physically behind black-framed glasses, a bumper crop of pimples, and a comfortably insulating chubby frame.

He is, in short, a prototype Art Bechstein, by age a kind of prequel. Like Art, Nathan is achingly alone, estranged from his entire family. His father is distant and disappointing and his love can never quite find its way to comfortable expression (which is ironic, given that he is a child psychologist specializing in troubled kids). His emotionally fragile mother struggles to find herself in the aftermath of her husband's affair, then their protracted divorce, and finally her own rocky return to the dating scene. After divorce adjustments are finalized, his younger brother, a would-be ally, must live in Massachusetts with his father and his new family. Across five increasingly painful stories, Chabon tracks Nathan's emotional development. In the end, at just sixteen, Nathan bids farewell to the soft prison of those imaginative retreats (pointedly, the Shapiro family lives on Les Adieux Circle). In counterpoint to Art Bechstein's strategic self-exile, Nathan accommodates the process of becoming ordinary, a decided shift from the too-easy (literal) flight of Art Bechstein. As such Nathan Shapiro is a harsh corrective to the fantastic—and seductive—extravagance of Art Bechstein. Unlike Art Bechstein (or Nick Carraway for that matter), Nathan Shapiro in the end accepts the unpromising materials of the real world, the ugly choreography of chance, and the fist-blow of surprise.[3] Nathan succumbs to Art's recurring nightmare: the boring, ordinary world where nothing happens with awful slowness; where passion quickly fades into the convenient and comfortable; where every gesture toward the saving comfort of community—friendship, family, love—twists inexplicably into betrayal and casual abandonment; and ultimately where the happiest moments thin quickly into memory.

When we first meet Nathan Shapiro in "The Little Knife," however, he is as carefree as any child heading for a catastrophe that they do not—indeed cannot—see coming. It is the summer of Nathan's tenth year. Loss is in the air, but it is distant, impersonal: his beloved Washington Senators have been unceremoniously moved to distant Texas. His family leaves Baltimore for their annual summer retreat in a rental cottage at picturesque Nag's Head in North Carolina's Outer Banks. Once they arrive, as his father checks them in for the week, Nathan notices outside the caretaker's office an old-style Coca-Cola vending machine that reminds him of a trip to New York City he had taken with his grandmother. Although only ten, Nathan admits to an inexplicable conflict of emotions—a "happy sadness, or, really, a sad happiness; he was too young . . . to have developed a sense of nostalgia" (131). This odd confession recalls, nearly verbatim, the ruminations of a much older Art Bechstein struggling to understand his burgeoning love of the beguiling Phlox, ironically enough at a beach. Sitting in the sand along the shores of Lake Erie at Cleveland's summer home, Art confesses, "I felt happy . . . at the sight of the fading blue sky tormented at its edges with heat lightning, and at the crickets and the shouting over the water, and by Jackie Wilson on the radio, but it was a happiness so like sadness that the next moment I hung my head" (*The Mysteries of Pittsburgh* 128).

The narrative voice-over here, however, quickly alerts us that something is amiss. Despite the idyllic ocean setting, there is tension: the parents' clipped exchanges, their muted arguments in other rooms, the mother taking her morning coffee alone, down to the beach. Indeed we are told that Rose has begun to explore new avenues of self-expression: she practices yoga; she has dabbled in Zuni mysticism and has investigated raising bonsai trees; and she has even pursued a real-estate license. These are indications, entirely lost on young Nathan, that she has begun a strategic movement toward independence. We only realize the depth of the couple's discontent when, as Rose dices celery to make egg salad, they quarrel over a kitchen knife they find in one of drawers. Nathan's mother admits to admiring the handy implement. The father casually suggests simply taking it, advice the mother rejects hotly with disproportionate irritation and a decidedly odd comment, "I'm not going to let you—make me—dishonest anymore!" (135). She then bursts into tears. We can only surmise that she is more than likely referring to an affair her husband has had or is having, an affair that would, of course, have already revealed his casual dishonesty and his insensitivity to codes of honor, a violation of their vows that would leave the mother feeling at once cheap and dishonest.

It is critical to Chabon that young Nathan has no idea what the problem is. He must watch helplessly as his parents fight in front of him, without apparent reason, over this trivial object. Later during a lonely walk on the empty beach, the socially awkward Nathan (his younger brother has already found kids to play with) impulsively fashions odd footprints in the wet sand using only the backs of his heels. He loves the anarchy of creating fabulous imaginary birds. He even fools his parents, who later try to guess what sort of creature could have left such weird tracks. Nathan delights in their confusion—after all, it is a kind of confusion he controls, a mystery to which, unlike the disquieting unease in the cottage, he has a ready answer. However, after their beach stroll, when his parents tell Nathan that the family vacation will be cut short, Nathan is sure that it is because of his deception and apologizes tearfully. He wants nothing so much as to understand conflict, to grasp the cause of the friction all around him even if it means accepting that responsibility himself. He is, of course, wrong. We understand the battling parents are simply weary of the pretense. Later while reluctantly gathering his things to depart the cottage, Nathan steals the little knife and sneaks it into his shoebox of treasures. He compares it, harmless there in his box, to a massive shark he had once seen in a diorama at a natural science museum—a threat contained, rendered impotent. He now controls the little knife that had done so much inexplicable damage to their vacation. Nathan is sure that the theft will lead to discord between his parents, accusations of who stole the implement. But that will be all right. Nathan actually relishes the imagined discord because he would be stage-managing a fight whose origins he understood, whose dynamics he controlled, and whose mystery he grasped. In this way, like Art Bechstein, he would be asserting desperate control over what is, in reality, a new and frightening experience.

The cycle's second story, "More Than Human," picks up the narrative line about a year later. The friction from his parents' irrevocable movement toward divorce has taken its toll. Nathan is a misfit who increasingly takes refuge within books. Even as the marriage begins its long-delayed disassembling, the father and son still spend every Thursday night making rounds to library branches and returning home with the backseat stacked with the science fiction Nathan has come to relish. On one of those Thursday nights, Dr. Shapiro decides to tell his son that he is moving out. As a child psychologist, the father understands the impact the news will have, and he regrets that Nathan must now be so rudely kicked out of the "perpetually expanding universe of nonsense" that is his safe-haven of books, the "soothing foolishness of words" (145). But he knows it must be done. On the way to their first library, the father abruptly pulls off the road, determined now to tell his son—but he cannot. Instead he invites his son to ask him any question. He hopes Nathan will ask about the impending divorce and promises an honest answer. Rather than engage such reality, Nathan, fed on a steady diet of science fiction, poignantly asks, "If I was a mutant . . . would you and Mom ever tell me?" (148). The father reluctantly admits that he would not. We see the implications: the father is too willing to leave his fragile, misfit son safe within a protective fantasy. Not surprisingly Dr. Shapiro never tells Nathan he is moving out. Days later, in a characteristic strategy of protection, the father dispatches Nathan to the local mall and then moves out his belongings. Nathan returns to find himself abandoned inexplicably to space (his favorite television show is *Lost in Space*). As he walks slowly through the stark emptiness in his parents' bedroom, he finds crumpled in a wastebasket a list of resolutions his father had apparently made years earlier, promises he had made to himself, promises to be more involved with his family, to live better, to be kinder—soothing, foolish words used to conjure a convincing fantasy. Dispatched to the trash, they underscore his father's new acceptance of limitations, his practical abandonment of the soothing foolishness of words. But Nathan is still caught up in that enticing foolishness. He is moved to phone his father and tell him that he is the best father in the world and that he could come home anytime. It is the epitome of the foolishness of words, distressingly naïve assessments so entirely divorced from reality that even the father does not buy into them and mumbles only a curt thanks.

A pattern emerges: moved achingly near the vulnerability of clear sight, Nathan retreats into the shelter of fantasy. Exposure to the painful reality of his father's ordinariness is at the very heart of "Admirals." More than a year and a half after the divorce, Nathan and his brother now ride with Dr. Shapiro and his new girlfriend, a bubbly nurse named Anne, to nearby Annapolis for an overnight getaway, a fancy meal, and a stay at a hotel. On the way Nathan reveals his new maturity and dedication to facts: in addition to clicking off state capitals for his own amusement, the four play a trivia game, identifying the artists on the pop-music station playing in the car. Nathan has a shining moment when he guesses correctly the artist of a particularly obscure song, "We Love You," as Eric Clapton. In command, the master of facts, Nathan glows. When the four stop in a pricey seafood restaurant crowded with more than a dozen distinguished-looking admirals, Nathan is shocked to see in the lounge his mother's new boyfriend deep in conversation, apparently with a date. In the face of such betrayal, Nathan, suddenly powerless and lost to words, feels like crying. As it turns out, understanding the real world is not like learning pop artists and state capitals. Anne leans in and gently tells Nathan that he had actually gotten the answer wrong, that it wasn't Eric Clapton but the Rolling Stones. Reeling, Nathan is now left shaken, uncertain.

As they all leave the restaurant, Dr. Shapiro pauses to talk to the owner of a flashy sports car (a millionaire playboy, Nathan imagines). Watching his father next to the flamboyant stranger, Nathan, in one of those unanticipated adolescent epiphanies, suddenly sees the father he has so long admired for exactly what he is: short, balding, disheveled, and nondescript, the kind of forgettable figure whom admirals and millionaires do not bother much to notice. As his brother laments, "He's only a psychiatrist" (165). Brutalized by fact, Nathan evacuates into a protective retreat. That night, unable to sleep, he escapes into an exotic fantasy in which he is the baby Moses newly set adrift in the bulrushes, his so-ordinary parents waving goodbye even as they sing the Stones' song, the boy gratefully emancipated from such unpromising parents, now destined for greatness. We see the poignancy. We recall from earlier that, as they had departed the restaurant, the four had stopped in a toy store and that Nathan had been transfixed by a carved figure of a knight crusader in a glass case—like Moses, a larger-than-life counter-personality to Nathan's real self. Like Art Bechstein, Nathan resists the threat of succumbing to the ordinary by fantasizing dramatically heroic projections.

Nathan's tender ambition to elude the ordinary quickly collapses. His first experience with falling in love, chronicled in the cycle's penultimate story, "The Halloween Party," involves an extravagant and sweetly improbable fantasy. Nathan has a crush on one of his mother's married friends, the deep-voiced, full-chested, chain-smoking Eleanor Parnell, a former professional golfer for whom he did yard work for years. Driving about town in her flashy red sports car, the woman is a striking exception to his mother's other married friends. Rumors follow her, apocryphal tales of desserts laced with marijuana and Christmas Eve trips to Vegas and long afternoons drinking wine while waiting for her husband, an Army major, to come home. Mrs. Parnell's past is as intriguing: her flirtation with athletic celebrity tragically ended by a freak fall from a horse; a failed real-estate business and a failed restaurant (appropriately specializing in spicy Cajun fare); and most poignantly the mysterious death of a baby some years earlier.

With his brother moved away and his mother now a nurse working long hours, Nathan increasingly envelops himself in growing infatuation, filling empty hours staring at Mrs. Parnell's photograph in his darkened bedroom and writing haikus and limericks to her in a freshman English course. Walking home from school one afternoon, he comes to Mrs. Parnell's assistance like the heroic knight he fantasizes himself to be: she is trying to rid her yard of a wasp nest by hosing it down with a garden hose. Nathan valiantly offers to take care of the nest. Of course he goofs it up, gets entangled with the bulky hose (with its phallic suggestion), and is attacked by a swarm of angry wasps. He and Mrs. Parnell must beat an inelegant retreat to a nearby field where they roll about for a moment, a strange interlude that convinces Nathan that he is in love. During their roll Nathan momentarily loses his eyeglasses, underscoring how he has gratefully slipped into the delicate blur of fantasy. When Mrs. Parnell gingerly dabs the stings on his thigh, Nathan has another one of those Art Bechstein moments: he is so happy, he cries.

Nathan resolves to declare his love at the Parnells' neighborhood Halloween party. Ready to forsake the childhood rounds of trick-or-treating (he must listen with irritation to his younger brother on the phone as he prattles on about his candy haul), Nathan rejects his first costume idea: the Marvel comic-book superhero Galactus, the World Eater, a fabulous creature of considerable power appropriate to the nerdy aspirations of an adolescent. Instead Nathan devises an overly clever conceptual costume: he will wear an ordinary business suit but fashion a hanger to suspend a light bulb over his head. When his mother quizzes him on what he is, he tells her he is a man in the process of having an idea for a Halloween costume. Before leaving for the party, Nathan accidentally falls on his glasses, breaking them. Undeterred he bravely declares, ironically enough, that now he sees with "particular clarity," that his eyesight is "cured" (180). Ready now, that is to say his vision out of focus, Nathan heads off to the Parnell house.

Approaching the front door, he rehearses his declaration of love, a by now "tortured sentence," a durable manifestation of the very foolishness of words (181). The evening, of course, is a disaster. Amid the adults with their exotic cocktails listening to their grinding disco music, Nathan glimpses Mrs. Parnell—she is costumed as Batman in a racy black leather bikini, black cape and mask, and fetish boots, suggesting an aggressive sexuality entirely unfamiliar to Nathan. He is suddenly exposed for exactly what he is: a nerdy kid at an adult party. Worse, he cannot hide, not even behind the costume. Mrs. Parnell does not understand his elaborate get-up. A lamp? A lightpost? Thomas Edison? In an effort to simplify the outfit, he removes the headgear and now challenges Mrs. Parnell to guess what he is. And he is, of course, (like his father) a nondescript guy in an unremarkable business suit, ordinary and unassuming and (now without the light bulb) metaphorically clueless. He asks Mrs. Parnell to dance. Given the dimensions of the evening's catastrophe, Nathan pulls a Bechstein: he retreats gratefully and too easily. Before they dance, Nathan puts his hand over Mrs. Parnell's eyes and her gloved hand over his. And there as the story ends in the reassuring and mutual darkness he clumsily arranges, Nathan obtains the courage to say "Guess who I am now" (185). Effortlessly, if gracelessly, he eludes reality and his own identity. Nathan's pattern continues throughout: exposure, retreat, exposure, retreat.

Only in the closing story, "The Lost World," Chabon breaks the cycle and completes Nathan's reluctant movement into the ordinary. It is a hot July night. Now sixteen, his mother recently remarried (to a modest geologist, a profession literally grounded in the real world), Nathan has just learned that evening that his father and Anne are expecting their first baby. Vulnerable, confused, angry, and reality closing in on him once again (recall Art Bechstein in the Pittsburgh hospital), Nathan opts to retreat, albeit this time via a more adult (and far clumsier) route: chugging four tall cans of malt liquor with three of his buddies, naked in a hot tub. Emboldened by alcohol and despite the late hour, the boys decide to cruise and stop at the house of a girl they know in school, Chaya Feldman, who has the reputation for being easy. It is time, they decide, for Nathan to get laid. Despite a pleasant alcoholic nullity, Nathan remembers Chaya, going to Hebrew School with her and playing games with her around the neighborhood. But as the lone virgin among the four, he agrees to be the one to knock on her back door. As he climbs the fence and begins his stroll across the Feldmans' yard, Nathan realizes he is still naked. But he relishes the feeling, even brazenly doing a quick lap in the Feldmans' pool. After an awkward moment at the door of Chaya's basement bedroom, Chaya recognizes Nathan and lets him in. We suspect that perhaps this evening, unlike the Parnell Halloween party, might mark Nathan's initiation into the real world, specifically the reality of sexuality. We assume the feisty Chaya, whose name is Jewish for "life," is exactly the wake-up that the man-child Nathan needs.

She is more adult than child and is, by comparison to Nathan, thoroughly grounded in the real world. She is reading Erica Jong's *Fear of Flying;* she smokes; she has travel posters instead of movie posters or pop-star pictures on her wall. She tells Nathan that she is leaving the next day for an extended stay in Israel, her father determined that she will learn her roots, her Jewish identity. In counterpoint, however, Nathan is already edging into a fantasy. He makes a typically awkward gesture by kissing her. Unimpressed Chaya coolly promises to write, which she literally does. She grabs a sheet of paper and hastily scribbles a note with a Smurf pencil, seals it in an envelope, and hands it to him. She makes him promise not to open it until she is gone. On the way back to his friend's car, reeling suddenly in the excitement of first love, Nathan nobly acts to safeguard the talismanic letter: he hides it in a neighbor's bird feeder. On the ride home, he engages in a vulgar variation of Art Bechstein's imaginative excess: he conjures for his horny buddies an entirely fictitious sexual encounter with Chaya replete with "sophisticated orgasms" until, overwhelmed by the betrayal of his beloved, he bursts into tears, recalling Bechstein's penchant for impulse-crying (203).

Convinced the mysterious letter is in fact a confession of love, Nathan is crushed when he returns for it the next day only to find it gone. Of course

Nathan does not require the actual letter to be catapulted happily into a romantic fantasy. He is now totally in love with the absent Chaya, her participation in the fantasy irrelevant, his love uncomplicated by any evidence. Sure that he has found love, he goes about "erecting all the necessary buttresses and towers and fluttering pennants in his imagination" (206). Weeks later he is surprised when a letter from Chaya actually arrives. He is in the kitchen resisting his new stepfather's attempts to broaden his horizons by having him try diced gherkin pickles in his lunchtime tuna salad. Although Chaya's letter arrives along with a letter from his father (who had never written before), Nathan wants only to read what he is sure is Chaya's declaration of love. He figures a neighbor must have found the letter and had finally gotten around to mailing it. He is crushed, however, when he reads the letter. Chaya says only that Jerusalem is terribly hot this time of year, that she has thousands of boyfriends, and that sometimes Nathan, far from a romantic interest, had made her laugh in school. She is, in short, casual in her interest and simply honest.[4] But that bluntness uncomplicated by subterfuge or tact is sufficient to finally shatter Nathan—he rips the note to pieces. At last, Nathan sees with painful clarity. We recall that in school Chaya had been known for her ability to sketch a realistic picture of an eyeball "with a sparkle on the iris, and fathomless pupils, and the finest tracery of veins" (189).

In contrast he is no omnipotent Galactus, World Eater; no suave James Bond; no swaggering knight errant astride a magnificent charge; and certainly no Moses destined to be Prince of Egypt. He is just a scared, vulnerable man-child who understands nothing, engulfed suddenly by the mysteries of Baltimore. Rather than evacuate into some improvised fantasy, he now accepts and surrenders. He consigns both his father's letter (a brief, coolly polite note in which Dr. Shapiro awkwardly tenders ineffectual clichés to reassure Nathan that he will always love him) and the torn bits of Chaya's note to a cigar box he keeps under his bed. For Nathan, life ahead will be crossed by perplexing mystery, a crushing cycle of expectation and disappointment, where love will prove insufficient, family distant, and the imagination useless. Without melodrama or hyperbole, Nathan simply heads to the kitchen, emotionally naked, resigned to begin a long life of gherkins in his tuna salad, an unspectacular adulthood in which nothing happens with awful slowness.

Veteran readers of Chabon, however, are understandably cautious. The stories of Nathan Shapiro surely reflect the deep frustration of their author at the time. Nathan's surrender leaves only a stark vision of life as a series of halfhearted and incomplete gestures, pointless and unfulfilling. Art Bechstein or Nathan Shapiro? Neither is particularly attractive. Such a deadlock inevitably reflects the difficult position of Chabon at the time, grinding away within the elastic confines of his own monstrous imaginative construct, the novel he could not finish. At this complex crossroad in his young career, Chabon could offer only two extremes: the exotic flight and faux-happiness of Art Bechstein or the heartbreaking surrender and crushing disappointment of Nathan Shapiro. But within just weeks of abandoning "Fountain City" and liberating himself, Chabon in a resurgent fury of creativity would conjure Grady Tripp and in turn tap a most significant and exhilarating alternative.

CHAPTER 4

Wonder Boys

Surprisingly (or perhaps not so surprisingly) for a novel that marked its creator's joyous return to the invigorating energy of narrative, *Wonder Boys* is populated by failed writers. There is Albert Vetch, an obscure hack writer of schlocky horror stories who, when the market for such pulpy fiction suddenly dries up, dispatches himself with a single clean shot to the temple. There is John Jose Fahey, a promising novelist who struggles for years to maintain relevancy until, when he is crossing a street one evening, an armored truck bearing the night take from a casino mercifully flattens him. There is the ironically named Happy Blackmore, who despite a hefty advance from an interested publisher could not sufficiently organize copious materials to ghostwrite an autobiography of an obscure Pittsburgh baseball player and who, years later, scratches out a spare living as a third-rate sportswriter and a luckless gambler. There is the perpetually stoned Sam Traxler, the stooped-shoulder, shaggy-haired former creative-writing major who now toils long, joyless nights as a janitor at the college from which he dropped out.

There is the bland if earnest English Department chair at the same college who collects expensive baseball memorabilia. He has spent years crafting a flakey study on the mythopoetic implications of the brief marriage between actress Marilyn Monroe and Yankee slugger Joe DiMaggio, an impenetrable exegesis that, at over seven hundred pages, has long struggled to find an interested publisher. There is the creative-writing teacher at the University of California at Berkeley who is haunted by his own early success, an exotic best seller that had been made into an entirely forgettable movie. Now with bad teeth and his zipper perpetually down, he delivers cynical, meandering lectures while staring absently out the window. There is the prestigious annual weekend university conference, dubbed WordFest, which brings together mercenary agents and blasé editors with earnest would-be writers, each toting the obligatory dog-eared manuscript or two or three. And there is even a loony dog, a blind Alaskan malamute, known for compulsively arranging bits of sticks in what appears to be a language, "almost intelligible hieroglyphic patterns,"[1] a message, of course, like those of Chabon's other frustrated writers, never delivered, never understood.

But chief among these failed writers is Chabon's narrator, Grady Tripp, a former wonder boy, a novelist of three well-received books who now awkwardly masquerades as a creative- writing professor at a small college in the cultural backwaters of Pittsburgh. A pothead, a heavy drinker, a thrice-married serial philanderer, Tripp clings to the fading celebrity of his early (and now largely forgotten) novels as he careens with indifferent recklessness into a massively empty midlife. It is a painful, sordid reality that barely troubles Tripp, having slipped so effortlessly into the enclosing superstructures of his own invention. Indeed long before he tapped the exotic energy of the imagination, growing up in a rural Pennsylvania town, he had been schooled in the sweet art of evasion. A formidable tight end in high school, Yeti-sized by his own description, he had been master of the gridiron, that harmless game-world of pretend confrontation and faux-warfare. Then after discovering Jack Kerouac before he was to start college, Tripp had hit the road with abandon and had ever since been gratefully hiding in a series of increasingly claustrophobic constructions conjured within his tireless imagination. (His last name suggests both his penchant for flight and his clumsiness.)

But if he begins Chabon's narrative like another Art Bechstein, entombed within the soft prison of his own model worlds, in a single momentous weekend, Tripp, like young Nathan Shapiro, confronts the unyielding edges of the reality he had so artfully evaded. First his wife, Emily, abruptly leaves him after discovering his current infidelity, an affair now in its fifth year, with Sara Gaskell, the chancellor at Tripp's college and the longtime wife of Tripp's boss, the chair of the English Department. But Tripp must also deal with the unexpected news that Sara is all but certain she is pregnant and is wrestling with whether to even have the baby, given her age (forty-five) and Tripp's precarious sense of responsibility. And Tripp must also handle the pressures stemming from the long-delayed visit of his literary agent of more than twenty years. Terry Crabtree, a decidedly flamboyant gay man, flies in from New York, his own job in jeopardy, eager to read Tripp's long-promised manuscript, a sprawling family saga called *Wonder Boys* that is a gargantuan mess: "nine central characters and a lifetime's worth of destiny" (133). It lays moldering in numbered boxes in Tripp's study, no closer to completion than it had been seven years earlier when Tripp had first conceived it. And on top of all that, Tripp must also sort through the implications of the unexpected discovery of an untutored talent, James Leer, one of his creative-writing students, a morose, socially awkward child-man raised largely by films. Leer's precarious anchorage in the real world has given him a remarkable felicity not only for storytelling but for pathological lying. He escapes effortlessly into made-up worlds of fantasy hometowns and imaginary parents while producing a prodigious stream of gothic tales largely inspired by old movies.

In short, for a novel roundly hailed as a delightfully fast-paced comic romp[2] there is something decidedly unfunny about *Wonder Boys,* an unsettling and, for veteran Chabon readers, too-familiar text-geography. Accidents brutalize the unsuspecting. Love sours with devastating quickness. The easy logic of suicide coaxes and little separates anticipation from disappointment. Any achievement is blunted by the inevitability of failure. Betrayal is the only expectation when the heart dares to venture outside its protective isolation. And amid the inevitability of such vast loneliness, the sole comfort comes from the cool, seductive solace of aesthetic artifacts—movies and books (in manuscripts or in print)—and from broader, far less subtle escapes such as recreational pharmaceuticals, prescription medication, and particularly alcohol. For Tripp, happily self-exiled for years within the ether of retreat, the darkest threats here come only from the truth: from occasional unguarded moments of honest insight, from accidental glances into unforgiving mirrors, through intrusive confessions from friends and family, or (as is often the case over this particular weekend) from surprise visits at his front door by dogged cops armed with questions.

At forty-one Grady Tripp is not so much a fraud as he is a fiction. He plays a responsible adult, a committed writing teacher, an important novelist completing a much-hyped and much-anticipated masterwork, a loving husband, an interested friend, a doting lover. Early on he dismisses with practiced cynicism even the idea of finding fulfillment in the ordinary, the everyday world that is Art Bechstein's harrowing, slow-motion nightmare and Nathan Shapiro's ever-encroaching reality. "I'd spent my whole life waiting to awake on an ordinary morning in the town that was destined to be my home, in the arms of the woman I was destined to love, knowing the people and doing the work that would make up the changing but essentially invariable landscape of my particular destiny" (45). Tripp is little more than a clumsily sustained performance piece, the inevitable product of retreat endorsed by Chabon's prototype auto-liberationist Art Bechstein. Appropriately, Tripp has constructed the perfect edifice for insulating himself from the small-scale terrorisms of the everyday: a formidable, forever-in-progress novel, so brimming with plots and characters that it may very well demand perpetual care. (Tripp notes that, now on page 2611, he is only on the fourth page of the work's original nine-page single-spaced plot outline). Bound to its reassuring bulk, comfortably numbed by his ever-present joint or tumbler of liquor, and sole proprietor of his private magic kingdom, Tripp sustains a self-indulgent free fall, content to stand apart and observe the quiet chaos of his life with self-gratifying bemusement. To quote Bob Dylan's Oscar-winning song from the 2000 Curtis Hanson film adaption of *Wonder Boys,* "People are crazy and times are strange / I'm locked in tight, I'm out of range / I used to care, but things have changed."

Chabon, of course, is more wary. He knows all too well after his own five-year interment within his own unfinishable manuscript that such escape is akin to committing suicide in self-defense. The guest lecturer at the university's WordFest describes in his keynote address how writers inevitably become their own döppelganger, a "malignant shadow who live[s] in the mirrors and under the floorboards and behind the drapes" (76). He observes that writers inevitably disconnect from reality, unconcerned, really unmoved, by the tragedies and joys of real people. They are content to observe and then recollect such second-hand experiences in the endlessly self-amusing play of language that, in turn, satisfies that odd craving for apartness, the security of dimensionless space. Tripp terms such disconnection the "midnight disease." Thus afflicted, he cannot conjure the requisite maturity to take seriously any of the roles he so entirely misplays: teacher, novelist, friend, husband, lover. He cannot bring himself to accept the responsibility of commitment. Even his car, a battered twenty-year-old, fly-green Galaxie convertible, is not his: he had accepted it as repayment for a loan he had given to a drinking buddy, who may or may not be the actual owner.

Uncomplicated by reality checks, Tripp can fall in love effortlessly and always fruitlessly. Despite the suddenly precarious state of his foundering marriage and the pregnancy crisis in his extramarital affair, he entertains an infatuation with one of his more promising workshop students, the beautiful Hannah Green, who is barely half his age and rents the basement of his house. He spends long hours in his study typing away with steady futility, an enterprise he engages with fierce devotion despite often comparing it to shoveling ostrich shit. And in ways that inevitably recall Art Bechstein, he compulsively simplifies those around him—colleagues and students alike—into easy two-dimensional cutouts. In bars, Tripp plays a most eccentric game, randomly selecting a patron, a total stranger, and with improvisational brio constructing a life-narrative for the person, transforming that person into a handy cartoon entirely for his own personal amusement.

But if Tripp begins his narrative safely enclosed within the world of his own amusements, by narrative's end, after a series of stunning, slow-burn epiphanies, he ultimately summons the nerve that Art Bechstein lacks to shatter that protective edifice and to assume the complicated responsibilities of engagement. Grady Tripp will touch authentic wonder in the very pedestrian world that so casually crushes young Nathan Shapiro. Veteran readers of Chabon will note subtle ties that Chabon introduces between the two: at one point, Tripp compares himself to Moses drifting in the wicker basket along the muddy Nile and at another describes his freshly rolled joint as being thick as a gherkin. But Tripp must first strip away the insulating layers of the persona he has so deftly created. When a stoned Tripp meets his literary agent at the Pittsburgh airport, Crabtree introduces him to Miss Antonia Sloviak, a tall, striking woman he just met on the plane and who is in town to visit her parents. Tripp immediately sees she is, in fact, a he, a transvestite—her disguise, like his own, a thin and paltry thing. Later that evening at the reception for WordFest, Crabtree becomes enthralled by the mysterious James Leer and ignores Antonia. In turn Tripp awkwardly offers to give Antonia a lift to her parents' home. As they drive along the deserted streets, Tripp watches as Antonia methodically sheds her outfit with practiced care. She first wipes off her makeup with dollops of cold cream, then slides off her black dress for a pair of denims, unfastens her black Lycra bra, and at last dons a modest pullover t-shirt. Now simply Tony, he is greeted with little fanfare by a decidedly nondescript father and a dime-a-dozen, charcoal-blue poodle at an unremarkable two-story brick home—the obligatory Blessed Virgin Mary statue standing in its plain front lawn. It is a moment, remarkably underplayed, of unforced and easy normality, without showy spectacle effects, a world without pretense, without melodrama, without the elaborate spin or forced touches of the faux-fabulous. It is singular moment, of course, entirely lost to Tripp. Only later does he embrace the liberating value of such pedestrian contentments. (We note that Tony, in contrast, lives on Liberty Avenue.) But before Tripp drives off, he observes, with typically practiced cleverness, that he must "rescue" James from Crabtree. Tony leans in and tells him with remarkable prescience, "You look to me like you need to rescue yourself" (97). Indeed amid the novel's often hilarious set pieces and the giddy picaresque feel of Tripp's lost-weekend adventure with its touches of slapstick, Chabon diligently works the serious business of Grady Tripp's reclamation.

From the opening pages Grady Tripp is clearly not well. He is overweight, unkempt, plagued by insomnia and bouts of nausea, and prone to blinding headaches and sudden black-outs, such physical afflictions manifestations of a something far more troubling. Like Art Bechstein and Nathan Shapiro, Grady Tripp is terrified by vulnerability. Like those earlier Chabon characters, he has no strategy to accommodate life's uncertainties. As a child, he grows up in the ramshackle country hotel his grandmother owned. His mother dies, just five weeks after he is born, from a staph infection she contracted while nursing him. His policeman father, a crippled Korean War veteran, commits suicide when Tripp is only four, devastated after he kills an unarmed college student by mistake during a routine night patrol. By necessity the young Tripp befriends an odd boarder, the pulp horror writer Albert Vetch, whose wife had been institutionalized after their two sons were killed in a freak fireworks accident. After Vetch's distraught wife commits suicide by throwing herself into a river, the young Tripp discovers the dead body of Vetch in his upstairs room, a suicide by gunshot. Given such multiple traumas, Grady Tripp has never been able to adjust to the harsh rhythms of misfortune, the implications of loneliness, or the cold intrusion of mortality.

He remembers as a young child one early morning watching his father through the half-opened door of his parents' bedroom. Coming off shift, he methodically stripped off his imposing police uniform all the way down to his boxer shorts. His prosthetic lower leg grew, in the child's eyes, ever smaller, frailer, more vulnerable, and more ordinary. "It was as though I were being permitted to see the crippled, balding, adipose gnome who dwelt within the brazen simulacrum, the lumbering golem I had learned to call my father" (91). The child is horrified. Years later, energized by Kerouac, Tripp does what characters in Chabon's fictions do best when pressed by such realities: he runs. In this case he abandons his education, his home, and his loving grandmother. Far from embracing spontaneity and the promise of a life as improvisation, Tripp opts to steadily entomb himself within his elaborate fictions. Even his three successful novels have featured, he acknowledges, luckless heroes who, unable to engage the world with confidence or integrity, have sought a variety of protective shelters—what he terms a "motif of burial and concealment underground" (235). And as he sucks deeply on the burned-out remnant of a joint, he observes without irony, "My heroes . . . were always trying . . . to escape from their terrible errors of judgment by crawling into caves and vaults and basements" (235)—a description that we (and Chabon) understand fits Tripp himself all too well.

As a first step, then, Tripp must be awakened to the dimensions of his charade. And so within the first forty pages, he is rocked by a series of shocks. Emily abruptly departs to her family's farm outside the city after her sister, who works at Tripp's college, tells her about Tripp's affair with the university chancellor. Despite her long struggle with infertility, Sara is nine days past her period and believes that the baby is Tripp's. But the most unsettling development is Tripp's growing relationship with James Leer. After finding out from Sara about the pregnancy during a reception at WordFest, Tripp steps outside to slip gratefully (and typically) into the easy escape of a quick joint and happens upon James, who is lingering in the moonlit shadows of the chancellor's yard. Earlier in the day, students in Tripp's writing workshop excoriated another of James's odd stories, this one about a boy molested by a Catholic priest. Tripp notes with alarm that James clutches a small pistol. Although James claims it is only a toy, Tripp suspects that the gloomy boy is more likely contemplating suicide. His stories are haunted by such melodramatic acts and, more to the point, the melancholic James, an inveterate lover of old movies, is known for his encyclopedic recall of hundreds of Hollywood stars who committed suicide.

Feeling awkward compassion for the quirky student, struggling for a distraction, and seeing the reception starting to break up, Tripp invites James to come up with him to the master bedroom to see something Tripp is sure the kid will find fascinating. There awaits the most valuable artifact in the massive baseball memorabilia collection maintained by Sara's husband: the black satin jacket actually worn by Marilyn Monroe the day she married Joe DiMaggio. Given Tripp's familiarity with the layout of the house and with the bedroom's sophisticated security system, it appears a simple plan. But as will become a pattern in Chabon's novel, Tripp's tidy plan, his plot as it were, goes terribly, quickly awry. While they are preparing to leave the bedroom, Tripp and James are confronted by Walter's dog, the blind malamute, who has long regarded Tripp with inexplicable hostility. The snarling dog clamps down viciously on Tripp's ankle. Before Tripp can even try to shake off the dog, however, James calmly shoots the animal dead—the apparently harmless cap pistol part of the novel's emerging tension between reality and fantasy. Only after their hasty escape from the house (Tripp simply stows the dead animal in the trunk of his car and downs codeine he unearths in Crabtree's luggage) does Tripp discover that James has in fact stolen the Marilyn Monroe jacket. Thus in short order Tripp must suddenly deal with the cataclysmic world of surprise and disorder.

The catalyst of this education will ultimately be the mysterious James Leer, whom Tripp more or less adopts for the weekend, a man-child so entirely devoid of secure contacts with reality that, like Art Bechstein and Nathan Shapiro, he simply concocts an elaborate imaginary life for himself.

He is Tripp's dark döppelganger, that part of him, the part of any writer, surrendered to the seductive imagination. James is never compelled to engage reality, effortlessly telling Tripp of his impoverished boyhood in a picturesque crossroads town he simply makes up. He is sustained by his belief that such confections are finer, somehow more real than the prosaic reality—his parents actually died in a meaningless small-plane crash, and he had subsequently been raised in comfort by doting grandparents in suburban Pittsburgh. Rather than accommodate that reality, James has turned inward, enthralled by the easy energy of storytelling stoked by endless hours interred within the cozy encapsulating faux-environment of old movies, especially the films of Frank Capra. (James clumsily used a needle to cut the director's first and last names into the back of his hand in tribute just after Capra's death earlier that year.) Given James's loopy resistance to any accommodation to the real world, however, his fascination with the iconic filmmaker—whose trademark movies always revealed an unshakeable faith in the essential worth of ordinary life—is darkly ironic.

In ways that recall the young Nathan Shapiro, James lives safety apart from the real, in a kind of box within a box. Along with Crabtree, Tripp visits the swanky suburban home of James's grandparents, a striking residence that resembles an imposing castle from some antique century, an "eccentric pile of fieldstone and shingles, bristling with awnings and trusses and pointy dormers that stuck out in every direction" (267). And James's basement bedroom is itself a veritable bunker rich with Gothic touches: a low-beamed ceiling, a cement floor painted to appear as if covered by a scarlet Persian rug, heavy curtains, elaborately carved furniture, and antique (albeit electric) candelabras. The centerpiece of James's basement-world, however, is a massive baroque canopy bed that resembles a "foundered galleon," underscoring the danger of James's gaudy free-float away from reality (269). Long-overdue library books are stacked all about his bedroom, the walls are hung with old movie posters and black-and-white stills of actors who have committed suicide. But most important is James's rolltop desk with its sturdy manual typewriter and the neat stack of single-spaced, typed sheets that measure his easy reach into the comfort of his own invented worlds.

Buried alive within such a chamber, James protects himself from the merest intrusion of the real world through the exercise of his imagination. Indeed the finished, novel-length manuscript that he lugs about in his frayed backpack is a sordid melodrama he has titled *The Love Parade* set in a rural Pennsylvania coal-mining town in the 1940s. Its flaky storyline splices lurid plots and stereotype characters from old movies. (He takes the title from a 1929 Ernst Lubitsch musical comedy that has nothing to do with the story's byzantine plot about a dysfunctional family that works in a mannequin factory.) James's plot touches on episodes of "sexual abuse, rape, incest, deer hunting, arson, the usual James Leer brand of mock-tortured Catholicism, suicide attempts, and the young hero's moments of ecstasy in the first row of the town's grand movie house" (248). No elements are even remotely drawn from James's own experience. When Tripp reads the manuscript, he of course finds it enthralling and terribly melodramatic (he reads the 250 single-spaced pages in a single two-hour sitting). But he also finds it "irremediably false," its rich period detailing and mannequin characters "crafted out of echoes and fragments and secondhand threads," a fiction produced "by someone who knew only fictions" (250). It is imaginative brio for its own sake, as if James were content "to raise, on the patch of vacant scrub that was his life, a teeming city of costumers, soundmen, hoplites, buccaneers, and Kickapoo Indians, where he could be producer and director, screenwriter and gaffer and makeup artist, the walk-on destined for stardom and the leading lady at the peak of her career" (251). It is a grand if empty illusion. We see the irony that Tripp can so honestly assess James's cavalier indifference to the real world yet his own gargantuan narrative is itself a blend of lurid and melodramatic turns that draw little on Tripp's own experience. The novel contains an "accidental poisoning, a car crash, a house on fire; the births of three children and a miraculous trotter named Faithless; a theft, an arrest, a trial, an electrocution; a wedding; two funerals, a cross-country trip; two dances, a seduction in a fallout shelter, and a deer hunt" (133). Ironically Crabtree, who in his careless quest for the novelty of new sexual conquests seduces the sexually un-oriented James over the weekend, reads the same manuscript but is impressed and decides immediately to publish it. He is certain that James will be the next wonder boy of the literary world.

The patent falseness of James's apprentice work stands as ironic counterpoint to the movement toward authenticity on which Tripp embarks. This becomes, of course, the subject for Tripp's narrative, which is the first-person narrative that we are reading. The trigger event in Tripp's reclamation is his impromptu visit to his wife's family farmhouse far outside Pittsburgh near the town of Kinship. Devastated by the revelation of Tripp's five-year affair, and in characteristic Chabon style, Emily has retreated there. The morning after the disastrous experience at the Gaskells in which James shoots the blind dog and steals the Marilyn Monroe jacket, Tripp's father-in-law Irv is intent on brokering a reconciliation on his own. He calls to invite Tripp to share the family's seder that night in celebration of Passover just as Tripp had always done in the past. Hungover and bleary and wary of such confrontations with the real-time consequences of real-time actions, Tripp clumsily declines.

Lighting up a charred roach and donning his lucky bathrobe (white chenille with pink and red geraniums on the pockets, an item that had belonged to a long-ago lover and that he now wears as part of his writing regimen), he happily pads off to his study and the protective enclosure of yet another long, and manifestly pointless, morning of writing. But in quick order he is confronted by increasingly threatening realities. First a police officer arrives at his front door and makes pointed inquiries into the burglary at the Gaskells and the disappearance of their dog. With inelegant half-sentences, Tripp dodges the routine questions and denies knowing the whereabouts of James Leer, who is at that very moment sleeping off the liquor from the night before on the couch in Tripp's study.

The visit shakes Tripp. Determined now to flee the increasingly tighter confines of the city, he enlists the groggy James for a road trip to Kinship. But on the way out of the city, he is momentarily distracted while waiting at a stoplight by a young family crossing in front of his car, the woman carrying a baby who wears a black eye patch. The baby appears to stare menacingly at Tripp. It suggests to him a pirate, a (typically fictional) figure that threatens imminent plundering and intrusive violence. It is for him a sign. He turns the car around and heads to the Gaskells determined to tell Sara about the dead dog and the stolen jacket and tell her that she must abort the baby, the easiest way out of the quickening complications of the pregnancy. It is, however, another of his neat plots that will go terribly awry. He finds Sara in her lavish greenhouse, surrounded by the lush growth of literally thousands of her carefully nurtured exotic plants, dressed in her mud-spattered gardening outfit, the very embodiment of an earth mother diligently engaged in the life-giving processes. She, not Tripp, takes command of the conversation, posing a simple ultimatum that discombobulates Tripp. Will he stay with his wife or commit to her and his child? Caught unawares, without conviction or thought, and despite his plan, he blurts out that he wants to be with her and not Emily. He immediately recognizes the inauthenticity of the declaration. He futilely searches his conscience for some authentic feeling to back his declaration of love, an "activity," he confesses, "never far removed from looking for a dead rat in a spidery crawl space under the house" (157).

Suddenly hemmed in by this new and far more oppressive reality, forced to accept the responsibility of engagement, Tripp does what Chabon's characters do all too well: he bolts. He promises Sara that he is off to Kinship to tell Emily, hastily kisses her goodbye, and heads back to his car. He and James then hit the easy escape of the open road. During that long drive to Kinship, Chabon entirely realigns the environment of the narrative. The tight claustrophobic gridlines of the city streets give way to sweeping rural backroads, unsnarled by traffic. The perpetual cloaking gray of the city sky, its needling cold, the steady drum of icy rain, and the hanging bittersweet smell of gasoline, river water, and burning tires give way to a green world that smells "cool and slippery like wet bark," great trees just beginning to bud under a cobalt sky and a warming sun (189). We recall suddenly that it is in fact April. Indeed when he first pulls up to the farmhouse, Tripp sees Emily's sister sunbathing, topless. In typical fashion Tripp does not respond to any of the stimuli and pays little attention at all. During the hundred-mile trip, he fires up a fat joint from his baggie in the glove compartment. Stoned when they arrive at the Warshaw farm, Tripp takes pains only to point out to James the family's pet cemetery adjacent to the rambling farmhouse, a "ragged stonehenge of whitewashed rocks" (169–170). He darkly notes the property's swampy backyard, sodden every year when the farm pond overflows.

Despite the obvious awkwardness over Emily and the revelation of Tripp's massive infidelity, despite the surprise of Tripp's presence after he had declined the invitation, and despite the fact that she has no idea who the quiet kid accompanying Tripp is, Emily's mother welcomes the two with unaffected sincerity. This is a significant change from the so-terribly witty, so-terribly calculated banter of the faculty reception the night before. Irene asks Tripp about his book without sarcasm (rare to this point) and welcomes James to their seder with grandmotherly warmth. By contrast James stays very much in character. He claims bafflement over a seder, ironic given that we will find out later he is, in fact, half Jewish. When Tripp first meets Irv, despite being obviously upset about his daughter (his eyes are red from crying and he has clearly not slept), the distraught father nevertheless literally ministers to his errant son-in-law: he rebandages Tripp's infected ankle in one of the novel's most compassionate moments.

The Warshaws quickly emerge as Chabon's first example of the difficult reward of engaging experience. They are hardly some perfect Hollywood-style mannequin family. The family has been sorely tested by commonplace tragedies the likes of which have never intruded in the baroque plotlines of Tripp or James. We learn that Irv and Irene years earlier suffered the loss of their only son in a drowning accident when he was just nine. But far from allowing such a catastrophe to drive them into despair, they selflessly adopted three Korean orphans (among them Emily), each the product of a difficult home life. And in turn each grown child has struggled with emotional catastrophes. Emily's nymphomaniac sister, the chain-smoking Deborah, has been divorced three times (most recently from a hapless dentist after less than a year during which he had been beaten up by the mob for running up gambling debts and then sent away to federal prison for income tax evasion). Her brother, the hard-drinking Philadelphia (he plies the unsuspecting James with beer most of the afternoon), who had long struggled in and out of juvenile detention before opting for the military and marriage, is a borderline sociopath who now keeps a massive boa constrictor in the farmhouse basement, regularly feeding it live chicks. And Emily, long considered the reassuringly stable sibling, now struggles with her own foundering marriage. But Irene and Irv willingly engage such difficult realities. Irene studied literature in college, yes, but as a reader not a writer, content to visit rather than disappear into such engrossing symbolic landscapes. Irv briefly studied classical music in college and had even written several avant-garde compositions in atonality before switching to the far more practical field of metallurgical engineering. Thus Irene and Irv, grounded in a quiet spirituality from their dedication to their Jewish identity, have maintained an enduring calm (a Buddha statue is present in their garden), raising a family of misfit orphans with patience, understanding, and care, forging from the inconsolable grief over a lost son a "loud, sloppy, jumbled-up, all-surviving family" (166). Perhaps the most critical difference between Chabon's book and the Curtis Hanson adaptation is that the film simply eliminates the Kinship interlude—Tripp arrives and is told Emily has gone to Philadelphia. But without the Warshaw interlude, the momentum toward Tripp's reclamation loses much of its depth.

Among such a committed family (who live just outside the town of Kinship, no less), the loners Tripp and James are decidedly out of place, only awkwardly participating in the family's Passover meal, itself a celebration (much like the Warshaw family) of the resilience of the Jewish spirit amid difficult circumstances. Not surprisingly Tripp invests little into the religious ceremony. He is more taken by Emily when she at last comes into the dining room—in form-fitting black jeans, her lips rouged and her eyelids inked—and reconsiders what he has come to the farm to do. But as the dinner ritual wears on with its richly symbolic foodstuffs and its carefully scripted prayers, Tripp, a lifelong indifferent Christian who looked upon his wife's faith like a baseball fan regards cricket, drifts off into a pleasing daydream in which he imagines himself (as Nathan Shapiro did) as Moses drifting among the bulrushes. Of course the pressing reality of Tripp's infidelity will quickly shatter this family gathering. Just as they are beginning to eat, Deborah will tell her sister about Sara Gaskell's pregnancy. Then in quick order virtually all of Tripp's carefully built safe havens will be similarly destroyed. First the mysterious James Leer is exposed. Irene decides the drunken James needs to go home. She calls his parents using a phone number she finds in James's knapsack and tells Tripp that the orphan boy is in fact from Pittsburgh and then his supposedly dead parents, or actually his grandparents, are driving out to the farmhouse to take their grandson home. "So the mystic lightning that tormented the dark sides of James Leer's fiction, all that sorrowful, cabbages-and-hell Slavic Catholicism, that too was also pure sham" (240). Then when Tripp returns to Pittsburgh, the grand illusion of his masterwork implodes. He finds out that the beautiful Hannah Green, his boarder who is also a promising writer, has read a large share of his massive manuscript (distracted by the police that morning, he had left it out). He asks her what she thinks, and she devastates him with simple honesty (recall Chaya Feldman). The manuscript collapses of its own weight, she tells him, the story lines have no discipline, characters fade to inconsequentiality amid pages of self-justifying description, the prose generating itself like some nightmarish perpetual-motion machine. She asks matter-of-factly with unnerving directness how much better the manuscript might have been "if [Tripp] weren't always so stoned all the time" when he wrote (302). Such honesty is "cruel charity" (303). Naturally Tripp grabs his manuscript and bolts.

In the meantime the police have taken James in for the theft of the Marilyn Monroe jacket. Tripp reasons he needs only to return the jacket, still in the back seat of his car, to clear James. But he finds that his car has in fact been stolen and surmises it has been repossessed by the shady character he had met in a bar the night before, most likely the car's actual owner. Determined now to help James and protectively toting his massive manuscript, Tripp enlists Crabtree to drive him to an empty sporting-goods store parking lot where the man he suspects owns the car may work. But an angry confrontation with the car's gun-toting owner ensues. As Crabtree tries to maneuver his car to help him, Tripp must watch helplessly as his unbound manuscript flies furiously through the open back door of Crabtree's car, out into the morning wind, a grotesque blizzard of twenty-pound bond. By the time Tripp jumps in and secures the door, only a handful of pages of his manuscript remains. It was his only copy, and Crabtree is oddly nonplussed. It is, he suggests, perhaps for the best. And in one of those epiphanies Tripp so often criticizes as hokey ("mystical fairy-fire" [21]) in the writings of his workshop students, he suddenly discerns that his own editor had long ago lost interest in him and in his masterwork-in-progress.

The model world of his manuscript so irretrevably gone, Tripp only now begins to turn to the solace of others. Crabtree leaves him behind in his car when he goes to prevent James's expulsion by returning the jacket to the chancellor in her office. A meeting is being held there to decide the boy's fate. Tripp's first inclination, of course, is to remain in the car, to escape the conclave entirely. He switches on the radio to polka music and lights a joint. But in the "tiny interval, between inhalation and blowing out," he is suddenly disgusted with himself (329). He resolutely heads for the chancellor's office and there dramatically accepts responsibility for the weekend's events. It is a moment of remarkable honesty and humility. Suddenly when he thinks of his lost manuscript, he thinks of the Gaskells' blind dog trying desperately to arrange sticks into a message. He collapses into a chair and cries. Momentarily lingering in Sara's maternal embrace, even as she lovingly plucks out his gray hairs, he hits bottom. He realizes that in a single weekend he has lost his publisher, his novel, his wife, his lover, his car, and his job. That sense of collapsing security is completed shortly thereafter during the convocation that closes WordFest: James Leer is publicly celebrated as the newest wonder boy. Tripp stumbles from the auditorium and, in a determined gesture of heroic accommodation, leans over the auditorium's stairway balcony and tosses his last baggie of marijuana down to the grateful, if confused, janitor Sam Traxler, the former creative-writing student. Even as he does it, however, Tripp feels dizzy. He is about to fall over the railing when, out of nowhere, someone hauls him back to safety. And the last thing he sees before losing consciousness is Sara's concerned face.

Recovering in a dim hospital room the next morning, Tripp is told bluntly by the doctors that his precarious health comes from stress and marijuana abuse, a toxic combination that underscores Chabon's larger thematic tension between engagement and escape. Like Art Bechstein in the hospital at the end of his narrative, Tripp still opts for the easy strategy of disengagement. He decides it would be best for Sara if he simply removed himself from her life and she abort their baby. On his way out of the hospital, however, he pauses at the nursery window and marvels at such stunning miracles of imperfection: their heads "dented, skin purple, and crazy with veins, spastic limbs struggling as if against some invisible medium or foe." Tripp confesses, "Boy . . . would I like to have me one of those" (352). But Chabon resists such a simple resolution. Tripp has too much baggage (underscored by the bulky tuba case he still lugs about, left in his car the night before by Antonia Sloviak). Dragging the tuba case, Tripp heads to Sara's house only to confront at last her husband, his boss, whom he has so ingloriously cuckolded. Toting a Joe DiMaggio bat from his collection, Walter lands a generous blow to Tripp's head even as Tripp attempts a lame apology. "You're a goddamn fraud, Grady. You've produced nothing at all since you've been here" (359).

The blow, however, effectively clears Tripp's head. He leaves the house and sits stunned and dazed in a cleansing rain, feeling "massive and buoyant" (362). He knows what he must do. With little ceremony, he slowly extracts the last surviving pages of his doomed manuscript from his jacket pocket, folds them neatly into a little paper boat, and sets them afloat in the gutter. He is at last free. In short order, Sara picks him up. He offers her a place to stay and gets into her car, leaving behind the tuba.

A younger Chabon might well have closed the narrative there on such forbidding uncertainty—indeed it recalls the close of *The Lost World* cycle. But here Grady Tripp, despite Walter's harsh judgment, does in the end produce something. In the novel's bright conclusion, Chabon affirms the quiet benediction of kinship. We learn that a year later Tripp and Sara have married and have relocated to Tripp's hometown. Temporarily impaired by the vicious bat attack, Tripp's vision has since cleared, and tellingly he has reclaimed his depth perception. Sara now serves as dean of the local college and Tripp teaches part-time. He writes a bit but relishes more the time he spends with his toddler son. He drinks, yes, but only beer cut with lemonade and even then only in the company of friends at the local tavern. He has entirely forsaken the dead-end isolation of marijuana. And above all he cautions his writing students against the danger of getting lost in their own fictions. Tripp achieves the life so feared by Art Bechstein, of ordinariness and routine where nothing happens, the compromised life of tuna-salad-with-gherkins that Nathan Shapiro so unhappily accepted as inevitable. Here the ordinary life can terrify and disappoint, but ultimately it lifts.

Of course, Capra-style happy endings can be problematic. A hard-core post-postmodern reader might search for irony, some indication Chabon wants to deflate what appears to be this unapologetic affirmation of the pedestrian rewards of kinship—love, family, work, community—that are so carelessly processed into clichés by talk shows and greeting cards. We feel guilty that a fictional construction can tap into the everyday world, which we so blindly take for granted. Imagine Chabon blessedly liberated from his own half-decade incarceration within an unfinished manuscript. Imagine, Chabon offers, such apparent surrender turning into liberation, such apparent humiliation into consolation, even triumph. That is, after all, the ancient wisdom of the Passover events that center *Wonder Boys*. In the end we must endorse Grady Tripp's exemplary recovery. In the end we must abandon the cruel folklore of the imagination and its fetching escapes that morph too easily, too effortlessly, into the claustrophobic nightmare of isolation. And thus we close what can be regarded as a kind of trilogy, the anatomy of the imagination described by a fledgling writer discovering both its energy as well as its complications. If we finish *The Mysteries of Pittsburgh* certain that the heavy bruising from encounters within the real world can be deftly avoided in a magic kingdom of our imagination, and if we finish *The Lost World* cycle bitter that it cannot be, we close *Wonder Boys* affirming a real world that is magic enough.

CHAPTER 5

Werewolves in Their Youth and *The Amazing Adventures of Kavalier & Clay*

But magic is an enchantment difficult to sustain. Even as Chabon was returned to the literary limelight, a wonder boy redux, even as he garnered wide critical plaudits for his second novel, he would return to the vehicle of the short story to test the viability of Grady Tripp's epiphany, exploring a darkening sense of the real world that Tripp so magnificently commands in that novel's conclusion. Given the stark testimony of the harrowing stories that he would gather in his second collection, *Werewolves in Their Youth* (1999), published just four years after *Wonder Boys,* Chabon did not become fascinated with the dynamics (or even the plausibility) of the Capraesque happy ending but rather the stunning moment of irrevocable realization, suggested by the bat swing to Grady Tripp's head, that delivers the often unwanted gift of clear sight and makes inevitable the movement toward accepting a difficult reality. These nine stories continued to test Chabon's evolving sense of the friction between the imagination and the real world, between escape and engagement. Characters in these stories have lingered too long within the pleasant shroud of denial, in worlds of their own construction. Now they must be hauled out in lightning-moments that strike like a blow to the head.

These stories thus provide critical counterweight to any assumption that Chabon tendered Grady Tripp's happily-ever-after lightly or naively. Indeed these stories, Carveresque tales shot through with trauma and anxieties, cannot sustain the lighter touch that so distinguished Chabon's earlier short fictions: wry, Cheeveresque humor; quiet, knowing irony; bemused exaggerations; and the reassuring touch of bearable closure. Should the breezy feel of the picaresque *Wonder Boys* suggest to a casual reader of Chabon that engaging the real world is somehow easy, Chabon used the stories published in and around the release of that novel to test the heavy implications of accepting life on its own terms without the gracious shelter of the imagination. Chabon here parallels that unexpected moment of enlightenment recounted in dozens of Hollywood horror films about the Wolfman. This is the specific moment when the unassuming central character, a man unaware (or in denial) of his own complicated makeup, is compelled to undergo the massive alteration involved in becoming what he really is. It is a radical and very real epiphany that is as necessary as it is brutal, for once endured it does not permit a return to any cozy assumptions held before. As always Chabon is engaged by the recognizable landscape of the ordinary. These are stories that anatomize the heart's blind hungers, stories of troubled kids, dysfunctional families riven by entrenched grudges, stale marriages collapsing into ugly divorces, failed businesses, the grinding malaise of long-term suburban life, and, perhaps most troubling, the propensity for violence among the suburban soul-dead.

The title story, for instance, centers on a nerdy, overweight junior-high kid who is taunted by classmates for his persistent body odor—despite excessive bathing, he smells like Campbell's tomato soup. He tries desperately and futilely to choreograph an awkward reunion between his divorcing parents only to witness in a most disturbing moment the two estranged adults caught up in a meaningless moment of carnal nostalgia. They make out on the couch, one of his mother's breasts hanging out, "loose and shaking and astonishingly white."[1] In another story, "House Hunting," a couple quietly drifts from each other despite a lengthy commitment to couples counseling. They desperately hope a change in scenery, a new house, might quick-fix their marriage. When they tour an upscale house (although it is, they are sure, way out of their price range), their seedy (and apparently drunk) real-estate agent appears far more interested in pocketing knickknacks from the house than answering any questions they might have. The couple begins to suspect the realtor might in fact be the former owner of the house, the estranged ex-husband of the woman now selling it. Uneasiness begins to build. The couple notices a business card in the kitchen with the number for the Domestic Violence Unit of the local police department. Room to room the realtor blatantly jams his suit pockets with an assortment of apparently randomly chosen items: a crystal animal figurine, a paperweight, a ping-pong paddle, a souvenir Space Needle, blue panties.

Momentarily (and inexplicably) excited as much by the agent's odd behavior as by a tube of lubricant they chance to find in one of the bedrooms, the couple impulsively makes love with animal fury (as part of their rushed foreplay, they each snarl how much they hate the other). The act—more a struggle than lovemaking—only leaves them empty and depressed. Suddenly they hear downstairs a violent argument between the agent and a woman. When the couple goes down to the kitchen, they find that the woman, they assume the agent's ex-wife and the current owner of the house, has taken a vicious swing at the realtor. (She is apparently upset over his presence in the house.) But now she is lovingly nursing the man's bleeding mouth. Without explanation of their violent confrontation, indeed pretending as if nothing is out of the ordinary, the woman calmly asks the couple whether they liked the house. The man, erotically (and inexplicably) charged by a glance at his wife's disheveled appearance, specifically her smeared mascara, responds enigmatically, "It's perfect" (51). The very Carveresque floating pronoun stubbornly refuses to clarify itself. What's perfect? Their lovemaking? The afternoon? The house? The wife's ruffled appearance? Chabon withholds any adverbial indication to clarify how the man says it—whether with sadness, irony, love, politeness, or anger. We are compelled to end the story thus suspended among possible readings.

In "Mrs. Box" Eddie Zwang is a Seattle optometrist haunted by the lacerating memories of a dismal marriage and a miscarriage years earlier. He is fleeing from creditors because his medical practice had been bankrupted by a long-shot investment scheme. He is now on the run in a station wagon loaded with stolen medical equipment that he intends to sell to start a new life in Mexico. He stops in Portland to visit his ex-wife's senile grandmother, who is deep in the shadows of Alzheimer's. He acknowledges how easy it would be to rob the old woman of her valuable jewelry collection. That night, when he assumes the old woman is sleeping off the vodka-laced dinner he had served, Zwang steals into her bedroom and purloins the jewelry box careful not to awaken the woman. But he experiences a most unexpected change of heart when, on his way out, he stumbles upon the sick woman, very much awake, sitting in a chair in the darkened kitchen, looking out the window and straining to see her old house. The optometrist is suddenly gifted with corrected vision. But Chabon will not sustain, much less reward, the warm fuzzy feeling of that all-too neat Capraesque epiphany. As the doctor looks out the window, he watches helplessly as repo agents who have been following him all day now slip into the woman's driveway, hot-wire the doctor's parked car, and quickly drive off. They take all of Dr. Zwang's possessions and his legal papers, in short, the last, best chance he had for a fresh start.

But perhaps the compelling "Son of the Wolfman," the recipient of a 1999 O. Henry Prize, best suggests the dimension and the direction of Chabon's evolution as a writer. Its theme—the harsh beauty of a world unadorned by the imagination—at once deftly interrogates and extends the logic of Grady Tripp's embrace of life's wonder in his Capraesque recovery of both marriage and fatherhood. "Son of the Wolfman" offers a wrenching look at the implications of our deep capacity for violence. Here a marriage is tested by a wife's decision to carry to term a child she conceives after being raped while she is out jogging. She is attacked by a notorious serial offender, dubbed the Reservoir Rapist. (In Chabon's increasingly paradoxical vision, the rapist is, in fact, a popular high-school math teacher and track coach.) Clearly Chabon is ready to grapple with harsher realities than the unfinishable manuscript of a midlife Peter Pan. Indeed the story offers a darkening world without access to the shelter-house of the imagination. Here there are no hard-core readers, no would-be writers, no accomplished artists, no quirky nerds, no quixotic dreamers. There is just the world as it is.

When Cara Glanzman, the victim of the rape, decides to keep the baby, Chabon records with meticulous fidelity her new-found maternal instincts and her careful preparations for the birth: she arranges for a midwife, enrolls in birthing classes, and embraces a healthier lifestyle to ensure an uncomplicated delivery. Such intense dedication to the health of her baby has a good effect on her. But it is *her* baby, as her husband, Richard Case, darkly intones. The reader glimpses Richard grappling in muted asides with the black rage he feels toward his wife's attacker and, more disturbing, the disgust he feels for her and against the unborn child, whom he terms a monster. For the first time in the ten years of their marriage, Richard feels alone. His carefully arranged world (he works as a television studio cameraman and is adept at the tidy packaging implied by tight framing shots) has been shattered by the intrusion of violence that has, paradoxically, provided the miracle of conception and the promise of life. This is all the more distressing to Richard because he and Cara for years struggled to conceive a child. Richard simply cannot fathom the painful irony of these staggering contradictions. He grows taciturn at work. He agrees to do photo shoots that are farther and farther from their home as a way to distance himself from the pregnancy. He attends to Cara's needs motivated only by duty, absorbed by a kind of self-righteous indignation. And in the last week of the pregnancy, he simply departs to stay with his brother. It is a gesture of callous retreat that recalls Art Bechstein and the unredeemed Grady Tripp, save that now the stakes are so much higher. Retreat is now indefensible, even cruel.

In the closing pages, however, Chabon pivots with provocative agility to the difficult business of Richard's reclamation. Weeks after he has departed, Richard receives a late-night phone call. The baby now two weeks overdue, his wife is desperate to trigger the delivery. She pleads with him to come home. He does, and she asks that he make love to her to stimulate labor. The gesture demands sacrificing his self-serving pettiness and his self-indulgent revulsion and accepting her and the baby as his responsibility, a moment of maturation that Chabon marks with the traditional image of blood-letting. Richard cuts his finger when he tries to slice open a tube of lubricating oil (ironically, he ends up in the hospital). Once at the hospital, however, Cara feels her contractions begin. Reluctantly, at the request of the delivery team, Richard agrees to catch the baby as it clears the birth canal. Unlike the moment of paternal bonding when Grady Tripp swells with easy love as he pauses at the hospital's maternity window, however, here there is no Capraesque happy ending. The baby has a thick shock of black hair, a clear mark of his paternity, and he gazes at Richard with pupilless, emotionless eyes. Chabon refuses to resolve into convenient simplification the heart-breaking uncertainties ahead for Richard, his wife Cara, and the child. The world cannot be as neat as Richard's television pseudo-world would have it. "Do you think he's funny looking?" he asks the delivery team, searching for confirmation of his fears and perhaps justification for another retreat. The nurse, who takes a photo of the newborn, is given the story's closing word, the single ambiguous utterance, "Beautiful" (82). We are light years beyond Art Bechstein's fabulous retreat, Nathan Shapiro's melodramatic resignation to gherkins in his tuna salad, or even Grady Tripp's hard-earned acknowledgment of the dangerous pull of the imagination. Throughout the stories Chabon gathered here, character psychologies are twisted, motives murky, emotions contradictory, endings ambiguous. These uncertainties presage the feel and tone of an ambitious novel that Chabon was even then completing, a work grander—and more forbidding—than anything he had yet attempted.

Although it is manifestly risky to interpolate back from a text to its writer, there is a moment of inescapable implications for veteran Chabon readers late in this landmark work, *The Amazing Adventures of Kavalier & Clay* (2000). It is May 1941. Joe Kavalier is a Jewish immigrant who, despite formal training at a renowned art academy in Prague before fleeing to America in the face of Hitler's rising aggression, has enjoyed immense success for nearly five years collaborating with his Brooklyn cousin. They created a series of staggeringly lucrative comic books about a superhero, inspired by the breaking success of Superman, whom they had dubbed the Escapist. Issue-to-issue the masked and stern-jawed superhero single-handedly defeats the insidious agents of evil stalking the European continent even as the real Hitler and his cohorts have grown menacingly virulent. As part of his new-found celebrity, Joe attends the Manhattan premiere of Orson Welles's monumental film *Citizen Kane*. So long enclosed in his comic-book world, Joe watches the film, taking in its scale, its audacity, its brooding atmosphere, its theatrical gravitas. He understands in a moment of bat-to-the-head clarity that the film had taken the basic premise of any comic book—the blending of commanding image and riveting story—to a scale that he had never dared. In a hard, crushing moment of insight, such a sweeping, magisterial achievement diminishes his work, despite its success, to trivia. The film demolishes Joe. As he ponders whether comic books are up to such scale, he realizes the doubts he has are not about the viability of comic books but rather about the viability of his own artistic reach.

And the same could surely be said of Chabon himself at the time. After nearly fifteen years in the public eye, scoring critical and commercial success with a series of relatively narrow fictions, domestic tales drawn largely from the precious reserve of his own experiences, Chabon was at something of a crossroad. He was successful, talented, and regarded as a consummate stylist with considerable verbal dexterity and lyric grace. But there was a nagging suspicion that he was nevertheless a lightweight, that his work lacked that ineffable sense of importance that defined major literary fixtures. Was Chabon ready to test the implications of his master theme—the imagination and its confrontation with bruising reality—on the ambitious scale he had assayed so disastrously in "Fountain City," his aborted epic of more than a decade earlier?

As it turned out, the answer was a resounding yes. *Kavalier & Clay* indeed brought scale to the Chabon canon with its formidable bulk (nearly 700 pages), dozens of named characters and its cameos by a gallery of historical personages (among them Orson Welles, actor Franchot Tone, crusading New York psychiatrist Fredric Wertham, New York governor Al Smith, First Lady Eleanor Roosevelt, and surrealist artist Salvador Dalí), and multiple intricately woven and highly engaging plotlines that shuttled deftly across more than thirty years and across three continents, including the frozen outback of Antarctica. With newfound maturity Chabon now explored the tension between escape and engagement on a cultural and historical scale. He tests Grady Tripp's hard-won faith in the kinship bonds of community, family, and friendship against a bloody century's darkest episode: the insidious rise of the Third Reich and its ghastly campaign to exterminate the Jewish people.

In shouldering that premise, Chabon moved well beyond his signature range, the small negotiations of misfit individuals who retreat to the splendid and intoxicating refuge of their full-throttle imaginations. Departing from the first-person narratives of his first two novels, Chabon adopted the voiceover of the omniscient historian. (He even provides numerous explanatory—and entirely fictitious—footnotes and comments on events that happened well after the narrative time, creating the wide-lens verisimilitude of a documentary.) The risks all paid off. *Kavalier & Clay* received glowing reviews and a shelf of literary awards, most notably the Pulitzer Prize. It was widely hailed as a significant departure for Chabon, striking proof that the now forty-year-old writer had at last come of age. The breakthrough work signaled important new artistic directions for its author, a wonder boy no more.

In defining this new Chabon, critics quite rightly lauded elements new to his fiction. For the first time Chabon, in his portrait of Jewish immigrant life in mid-century New York City, brought to the fore a deep investment in his own religious roots, a reclamation, even rediscovery, of the dimensions of Jewish identity and its meaning in a contemporary and often hostile world. (By contrast, in *The Mysteries of Pittsburgh,* Art's religion is at best an aside; and the seder set piece in *Wonder Boys* is more a sharply drawn comedy of manners.[2]) In addition to praising the new interest in Jewish identity, critics hailed how Chabon for the first time frankly and forthrightly investigated the moral and psychological dilemma of coming to terms with gay identity through the character of anguished comic-book writer Sammy Clay. By contrast Arthur Lecomte's homosexuality was never tested. Indeed the flamboyant Lecomte relishes the bohemian freedoms that such nontraditional identity brings. Art Bechstein terminates his flirtation with bisexuality by literally flipping a coin. And the side story of Terry Crabtree's casual weekend seduction of the virginal James Leer is at best a cautionary aside amid the much grander parable of Grady Tripp's reclamation.

Critics also commended how, for the first time, Chabon introduced scale to his fiction, managing nothing less than a cultural biography of three decades of the American century, a meticulously researched old-school tome that drew (by Chabon's admission) on model-texts of nineteenth-century historic realism such as George Eliot's *Middlemarch* and, particularly, Leo Tolstoy's towering *War and Peace.* Critics noted that Chabon expertly executed that classic genre's panoramic feel, its enthralling sense of storytelling, and its self-consciously generous detailing (most sumptuously in the re-creation of jazzy New York City, just awakening from the Great Depression and rediscovering elegance in the short months before Pearl Harbor). And finally critics lauded how, for the first time, Chabon steeped himself in something other than the scratch materials of his own autobiography. He offered with meticulous verisimilitude (a three-page Author's Note acknowledged the range of works researched) a presentation of a neglected period in American popular culture: the golden era of American comic books that improbably coincided with the emergence of the Nazi menace in Europe, an era far removed from Chabon's signature contemporary narrative settings.[3]

Critics noted that the usually wry Chabon, in highlighting that era, had added a keen new tonal edge to his fiction: genuine outrage. He vented his indignation over the exploitation of these first-generation creators of classic comic-book heroes, most of them lightly educated Jewish immigrants. Joe Kavalier and Sammy Clay, for instance, sell all the rights to the Escapist to predatory publishers for a paltry $150. Over the next twenty years they watch as the comic books sell millions and later the character is optioned first to radio and then to movie serials and eventually to television and even commercials. To capture the feel of comic books, Chabon was further applauded for his ability to conjure comic book characters without recourse to the visual dimension typical of the genre, making those creations vivid to the reader through language alone. In mesmerizing chapters rich with appropriately elevated prose, Chabon gave the back stories of the comics series' three main characters in the fictitious metropolis of Empire City. Tom Mayflower, the crippled magician's assistant, becomes the Escapist and vows to rescue "those who toil in chains of tyranny and injustice."[4] The manic bomb-throwing archvillain known only as the Saboteur, the Vandal Supreme, each night creeps forth from his shadowy laboratory lair beneath the city and selects random targets, waging endless war on the very infrastructure of the metropolis, unnerving the populace and creating a perpetual state of unease. And Judy Dark, the mousey and bespectacled Under-Assistant Cataloguer of Decommissioned Volumes in Empire City's public library, one night interrupts a robbery in progress (of an enchanted book of magic). During the ensuing chase, when a live wire is dropped into a rain puddle sending a bolt of energy through her, she is transformed into Luna Moth, a full-breasted crime fighter gifted with enormous green wings and the ability to stun criminals with blasts of green energy rays.

Jewish identity? Gay rights? Tolstoyan scale? American cultural history? Outrage over the inequities of capitalism? Fabulous comic book characters with flamboyant backstories? Certainly these elements seemed radically new for Chabon. Yet they very much served to underscore what had long been the centering concern of *Kavalier & Clay.* In following the creative collaboration of the aspiring writer Sammy Clay and the classically trained artist Joe Kavalier, the novel represents less a radical departure for Chabon and more a signal evolution in his decades-long testing of the viability of the artist's imagination and its seductive offer of grateful retreat. Chabon investigates this tension now against the wide-screen of a brutal and graceless age. Within his narrative, gaudy comic books celebrating the triumph of good over evil in fabulous (and entirely symbolic) inkscapes must vie with forbidding headlines that testify to the reach of evil and the impotency of good in the real world. Chabon's assessment of America at mid-century significantly tempers any sunny Capraesque optimism. The novel's opening chapters take place in the years just before Pearl Harbor, in an America still crippled by economic catastrophe caused by the colossal greed of the privileged few. The nation is mired in entrenched myopic isolationism and miscalculated neutrality that allows Hitler to catapult to power in Germany virtually unchallenged. Then the novel shifts to the war years with its steadily accumulating record of Boschian atrocities and violence as well as its disturbing undercurrents of rampant jingoism and ethnic hatred. The novel closes in the mid-1950s where, amid the upholstered complacencies of America's emerging suburban model worlds, a cabal of ruthless far-right demagogues conducts ruthless inquisitions designed to quash any assertion of nontraditional ideas, a relentless campaign of slander and innuendo that in turn sustained a tense national environment of intolerance, paranoia, and fear.

Clearly Chabon fears that in such an era, amid such an oppressive reality, the imagination cannot succeed. What good can the fabulous creatures of the imagination, ink printed on paper, do in a real world that must, generation to generation, bear witness to our apparently infinite capacity to wound each other? As Sammy Clay gushes in what would become the mantra of their superhero, "To all those who toil in the bonds of slavery, and . . . the shackles of oppression, [the Escapist] offers the hope of liberation and the promise of freedom." The Escapist is conceived as good empowered, part Houdini, part Robin Hood, part Albert Schweitzer. The cover of the first issue of Kavalier and Clay's *The Escapist* in late 1939 features the costumed superhero landing an "immortal haymaker" on a stunned Adolf Hitler, his jaw "trailing a long red streamer of teeth" (150). It shocks of course. The timid investors balk, fearing a backlash because America and Germany were not at the time technically at war. They demand fictionalizing the German chancellor as Attila Haxoff, the Nazis as the Razis, Agents of the Iron Chains, the Allies as The League of the Golden Key, and Germany as Zothenia. But as history so powerfully testifies, such richly imagined narratives, such bold and entirely fabulous creations, do little good, are little more than flimsy shelters to forestall confronting the bleak realities all around.

Thus for all the elements new to Chabon's work, characters here test the powerful (and familiar) persuasion of escape and the coaxing strategies of denial. They succumb to familiar and attractive evacuations: retreating to movie theaters, indulging in drugs and alcohol, maintaining secrets and false identities, engaging in prolific storytelling, abandoning families and careers, and even physically going into years of hiding. But by narrative's end, the reach of the imagination and the logic of escape is, finally, too limited. Chabon counsels the need, amid the larger obscenities of the twentieth century, to nevertheless embrace the everyday, the difficult complications of love, the imperfect wonder of family, and ultimately the unforgiving absolute of death itself. In this the novel surely recalls the tender closing epiphany of Grady Tripp except that here such complicated affirmation is rendered within the crucible of a world—rather than a private life—gone to hell. Imagine if, in a sequel to *It's a Wonderful Life,* Frank Capra had decided to dispatch the redoubtable George Bailey to Bergen Belsen.

As its title suggests, *Kavalier & Clay* is structurally a contrapuntal narrative, unlike Chabon's earlier novels that had each maintained a clean and centered focus. Here we follow the complementary narratives of two cousins who, like the superhero they collaborate to create, are all too adept at escaping when harsh realities press too closely. Josef Kavalier actually studied under the master Houdini and late in the narrative visits the magician's elaborate Long Island tomb. It is Chabon's argument, however, that both escape artists must in the end abandon such willful strategy of self-preservation and prepare, hesitatingly, to engage the most amazing adventure of all: the day to day. For all its evident interest in Jewish identity and gay rights and even the economic inequities of the early years of the comic book industry, the narrative is haunted (as Chabon's epigraph suggests) by the ghostly presence of an eccentric character drawn from classic nineteenth-century American literature. In Hawthorne's strange little tale, a man named Wakefield, living in London, impulsively decides under the pretext of going away on a business trip to simply leave his wife. He stays gone for nearly two decades, living within a block of her, watching her go about the business of grieving and settling into complacent widowhood only to find, after so many years had passed, that he cannot bring himself to return to his wife.

The premise gives Hawthorne the opportunity to ruminate on the tension between escape and engagement, between the fancy and the heart, and how the wretched man in electing exile has risked losing his place forever, becoming the Outcast of the Universe. The story closes on a most ambiguous note. One rainy autumnal evening, on his customary walk through his own neighborhood, Wakefield simply decides it is time to return home. Wet and shivering, he slowly ascends the steps to reunite with the wife he abandoned two decades earlier. We are not given the reunion itself—Hawthorne is unwilling or unable to chart the difficult reentry. Without a word Wakefield simply passes across the threshold once the door opens. Thus we are left in a most perplexing uncertainty. With its interrogation of the lure and the dangers of self-exile, "Wakefield" provides a telling commentary on Chabon's many self-exiled characters and measures, given its cautionary tone, how a mature Chabon is prepared now to test the implications of that difficult, necessary return without the tidy (and reassuring) ending typical of his earlier works.

The narrative begins with the gripping backstory of Josef Kavalier. Born to privilege in Prague (both his parents were doctors), a practicing magician and auto-liberationist as well as an accomplished illustrator, Josef is smuggled out of Hitler's Czechoslovakia. He spends twenty-seven tortuous hours in a trick coffin designed to secret out of the occupied country the legendary Golem, the imposing totemic figure fashioned from the silty clay of the River Moldau more than four centuries earlier by a mystical rabbi. It is believed to come to life whenever the need arises to protect the Jewish faithful from persecution (and it will eventually become the model for Joe's superhero). For the first time in his fiction, Chabon in the character of Josef Kavalier tests the will of the vulnerable and helpless who are brutalized not by collapsing marriages or dead-end jobs but rather by the formidable currents of world events and who, despite the enormity of the odds, resolutely engage those forces. When Josef escapes Prague, he does so knowing he must leave behind his family: his parents, his ailing grandfather, and most painfully his younger brother, Thomas. Before he leaves, he repeatedly promises them that they will all meet again at the "Statue of Liberation." Once in Brooklyn, Josef (now Joe) agrees to help his cousin with his long-shot comic-book scheme, which he views merely as a promising way to secure money to arrange his family's passage to safety. (As a classically trained artist, Joe disdains the slap-dash drawings typical of the genre.)

Whatever success his comic books initially enjoy, Joe cannot forget the family he was forced to abandon. He uses the comic-book narratives to fight the war, against which he is so helpless, in the real world. In October 1940, after securing a publishing contract for the comic book, Joe spends a most satisfying (if sleepless) week in an obscure corner of his comics studio drawing his way to a quick and dramatic end to the war, which is in actuality only in its first bloody months. In Joe's heroic narrative, the Escapist flies to war-torn Europe aboard his autogyro and dukes it out with an entire division of the Wehrmacht. "In a transcendental moment in the history of wishful figments," he captures the suddenly pathetic Führer and drags him before an international justice tribunal (166). The villainous dictator is summarily executed, inaugurating an unprecedented era of world peace and, of course, the freeing of "the imprisoned and persecuted peoples of Europe—among them, implicitly and passionately, the Kavalier family of Prague" (166). Safe within the gravitational field of his imagination, Joe feels contented, alive, and hopeful. But Chabon cautions that it is a flimsy shelter. Even as his flamboyant fantasy is printed, lashed in thousands of bundles for sale on the street corners of New York City, Joe listens to the radio and hears reports of new legislation in occupied France that will enable the relocation of the nation's Jews to Nazi labor camps. Deflated, frustrated, profoundly ashamed, he bangs the crown of his head against the window frame in his studio until a thick knot swells. "The Escapist was an impossible champion, ludicrous and above all *imaginary,* fighting a war that could never be won" (168).

Given Grady Tripp's stumbling movement toward the reanimating energy of love and the consolations of marriage and family, Chabon not surprisingly tests that same dynamic here. He gives the brooding and stoic Joe Kavalier the chance to fall in love. Committed to the sixteen-hour work days necessary for the fledgling comic-book enterprise as the only way to earn the money he needs to secure his family's freedom, Joe diligently denies himself any pleasures. With monkish intensity, he does not carouse, does not drink, seldom leaves the studio, and never even talks to women. But when Joe first meets the exotic (and extravagantly named) Rosa Luxemburg Saks, an avant-garde artist currently toiling as a magazine photographer, he is immediately compelled by inexplicable certainty that in Chabon's fictions commences the arc of a love affair. It perhaps helps that she is naked, sleeping in the empty apartment where Joe and his friends have decided to work up the pitch for the new comic book. Despite his enchantment with the mysterious beauty, it will be more than a year before Joe actually talks to her—but he never forgets her. Given the template of Grady Tripp, we are certain that Rosa, so passionate, so unpredictable, so, well, artistic, can be the instrument of Joe's salvation. At a party of Manhattan's avant-garde community centered on a visit by the surrealist icon Salvador Dalí (with typical flair, the eccentric artist comes to the party dressed in a deep-sea diving apparatus complete with a globular helmet and noisy gas-powered air pump), Joe watches the feisty Rosa work the room, made up predominantly of men, telling ribald stories with effortless energy, playing with abandon on the shock value of the word "fuck." He is mesmerized and at last introduces himself. When Dalí's diving suit malfunctions later in the evening, the quick-thinking Joe (trained as an escape artist) frees the gasping artist and becomes, in turn, a kind of real superhero. Impressed Rosa invites Joe to her nearby studio apartment to see her artwork. He agrees—the studio is cluttered, exultantly decorated by, among other original objets d'art, Georgia O'Keeffesque erotic renderings of ordinary food. The apartment building has a moth infestation: they fleck the walls and flit all about the tiny apartment in a kind of large-scale performance art piece. (Rosa later becomes the model for the comic book's sexy female superhero, Luna Moth). Rosa's liberated sexuality ignites Joe's long dormant libido. But even after they consummate their fiery attraction, even as he finds himself spellbound just watching her work at her easel (she is for him an "inexhaustible source of wonder" [324]), nothing eases his guilt over his abandoned family. Tripp-esque love, Chabon cautions, cannot sustain.

In fact Joe spends two frustrating years early in the war besieging the German Consulate in New York City to obtain information about his family from the scant records available from occupied Czechoslovakia. He haunts the docks, wandering among the throngs of immigrant families reuniting under the striped awnings of the gangways: "It was like a noseful of wine that he could not drink; yet it intoxicated him" (182). During one of the routine visits to the consulate, a bureaucratic lackey, the Adjutant for Minority Relocation, informs Joe with chilling indifference that Joe's father had been reported dead from pneumonia weeks earlier while under house arrest in Prague. In turn Joe decides that the seductive escape into his comic books, where two-dimensional superheroes reliably triumph over cutout villains, is simply not viable. He will engage reality. He will fight the real war. Uncertain whether he can enlist in America because of his immigrant status, he impulsively jumps into his car and heads to Canada, intent on joining the Royal Air Force. But guilt again stops him. He knows he must return. He may not be the Escapist, able to win the war singlehandedly, he thinks, but he can rededicate himself to rescue what was left of his family.

Still angry and spoiling for a fight, Joe returns to the city. He spits at the polished shoes of a vaguely German-looking man waiting on a subway platform. Later he breaks into the offices of the Aryan-American League, a prominent ethnic pride organization in a heavily German neighborhood in the Upper East Side. When he discovers a file on the Escapist that decries it as crass anti-German propaganda, he is driven to vandalism. But these are gestures, ineffective and narrow. Desperate to save his brother as the war drags on, Joe musters his amassed wealth and his political connections. Through a relief agency that Rosa knows, he arranges for a boat out of Portugal to bring 324 Jewish refugee children—among them his brother Thomas—from central Europe to America. The unarmed boat is christened *Ark of Miriam* after the sister of Moses who saved her helpless infant brother by putting him in the wicker basket to evade the Pharaoh's proclamation to kill all first-born, male Hebrew children. Shortly after leaving Portugal, the refugee boat is torpedoed by a German U-boat. The desperate captain must set the children out in lifeboats. But a freak storm renders any organized rescue impossible, and all the children are lost at sea. Hearing the report, Joe is shattered. He summarily abandons Rosa (who is, although he does not know it, pregnant) and Sammy (as well as their thriving comics business) and heads to Newport, Rhode Island, to join the Navy. He is intent now on killing Germans in real time, to break free of the intoxicating shelter of the Escapist's elaborate fantasy.

But Joe ends up stationed along with a handful of other sailors in the arsenic-white wastes of Antarctica, there to track German U-boat movements in the Atlantic and to monitor enemy radio chatter. A fluke malfunction in the radio shack's stove kills all but Joe and a pilot. Joe diligently continues to monitor the radio and eventually contacts another subarctic outpost, more than eighty miles away. It is manned, he discovers, by a lone German soldier, an army geologist. Seeing at last a chance to engage the war firsthand, a chance to strike at the Third Reich, and despite standing orders not to engage the enemy unless directly attacked, Joe darkly determines that he will kill the geologist to avenge the death of his brother. The gesture recalls the melodramatic simplifications of a comic book. The flight across the rugged arctic wilderness that separates the two camps, however, is hardly a superhero spectacle. The pilot's appendix ingloriously bursts, and he dies when the plane crash-lands. Nevertheless Joe struggles across the remaining miles to the German's camp and at long last has his showdown. The two exchange shots and Joe finally kills a Nazi. Such heroics, however, provide none of the comic-book grandeur: this is reality, shoddy and untidy. Joe feels only a devastating guilt and even tries to minister to the dying geologist.

And in the spring when Joe is at last rescued, he is still burdened with the guilt over his family's fate. He cannot bring himself to return to his old life and opts, like other Chabon signature characters, to affect a grand escape. He slips through the post-war troops returning stateside through Cuba and makes a circuitous return to New York City where he entombs himself in the Empire State Building undetected, à la Hawthorne's Wakefield, within walking distance of his cousin's comics business. "Having lost his mother, father, brother, and grandfather, the friends and foes of his youth . . . his history—his home—the usual charge leveled against comic books, that they offered *merely an easy escape from reality,* seemed to Joe actually to be a powerful argument on their behalf" (575). For nearly ten years Joe seldom leaves the rented office he maintains on the seventy-second floor (a front for a business that claims to sell vanishing cream). With the eccentricity of a recluse, Joe amasses thousands of comic books that surround him in his office like a bunker. To ensure the viability of his escape, he dons outrageous disguises whenever he ventures out into the Manhattan streets. Like Grady Tripp, Joe occupies his time working tirelessly on what becomes an enormous, ambitious manuscript, a grandly conceived graphic novel, more than two thousand pages, about the Jewish Golem itself, work that becomes therapy for the melancholic Joe, crucial to his eventual reengagement of the world. "All the grief and black wonder that he was never able to express, before or afterward . . . all of it went into the queasy angles and stark compositions, the cross-hatchings and vast swaths of shadow, the distended and fractured and finely minced panels of his monstrous comic book" (577–578).

Like Grady Tripp, Joe will in the end forsake that imprisonment. Learning that Sammy and Rosa have moved to a Long Island suburb and are raising Tommy, the child he suspects is his, Joe makes tentative (and secret) contact with the boy, now eleven years old, meeting him initially in a neighborhood magic store and introducing himself as a cousin he didn't know he had. The boy is determined to reintegrate his cousin into the family even as Joe has concocted a most dramatic return for himself. Tommy types an anonymous letter to the city's principal newspaper dramatically announcing that the Escapist will leap from the Empire State Building to draw attention to the plight of the artists and storywriters who never shared in the royalties that comic books earned. The letter is published and, amid the buzz created by what most (including Sammy) assume is some kook involved in a publicity hoax, Joe, dressed in an old Escapist costume, climbs to a ledge more than eighty floors up, nearly a thousand feet above the city. There he is finally reunited with Sammy who, desperate to stop the stunt, points out that their superhero, while gifted with strength and courage, could never fly. But throwing his arms out wide, Joe steps free and, suspended only by an unseen complex of rubber bungee cords, drops to the relative security of a ledge two floors down. It is a richly symbolic fortunate fall for the voiceover authority: "Joe had failed to get out of his self-created trap; but now the love of a boy had sprung him, and drawn him at last, blinking, before the footlights" (556).

Redeemed by the love of his son and now reengaged by the need for family, Joe in the closing chapters determines that the wealth he has squirreled away (close to a million dollars) can help reestablish the creative dynamo that was once Kavalier & Clay, beginning with his own ambitious graphic novel on the Golem. Over the ten years that his cousin has been married to Rosa and raising his son, the hard-luck Sammy worked through several failed business ventures and now toils as a low-level storyboarder in a third-rate comic-book house while the once-promising artist Rosa, now thirty five, cranks out gushy romance comics to help bored housewives escape suburban purgatory. Joe is determined at last to affect a genuine rescue. But Chabon understands that it will be far more difficult than the abject apologies Joe humbly tenders to both Sammy and Rosa. The boy, Tommy, knows only that he is adopted; he has no idea that his newfound cousin is his father. Traumatized as a child by his own father's cold abandonment, Sammy understands the broader implications of Joe's return—and it is not about reinvigorating business opportunities. He knows his cousin will have to work to rebuild his family—and in that endeavor Sammy knows that he will only be in the way. In the early morning while Rosa and Tommy and Joe are sleeping, with suitcase in hand, Sammy slips quietly out the back door of the suburban house that was never really his home. He heads off to California and the promise of finding work in the burgeoning television industry. Chabon tenders the thin hope that the long-suffering Sammy might find some measure of contentment.

The story of that difficult search for contentment forms the other braid in Chabon's contrapuntal narrative. It is all too easy for Sammy Clay to slip from the reader's attention. In the opening chapters, after following the harrowing tale of Josef's dramatic escape from Nazi Europe hiding in a coffin in the hold of a transoceanic ship, readers experience an inevitable let-down when we then meet his Brooklyn-born cousin. Samuel Klayman is a mild-mannered clerk at Empire Novelty Company (specializing in whoopee cushions), a nerdy dreamer (he yearns at turns to be a great writer or perhaps a great doctor), a man-child who at seventeen, his education dead-ended, now lives with his mother in a cramped Ocean Avenue tenement with few expectations save the flimsy stuff of his fantasy ambitions. His life is an empty place in which nothing happens with awful slowness. Compared to the courageous transoceanic escapades of his cousin (who is even gifted with a swashbuckling name), Samuel offers a far quieter, far less gaudy narrative—like an old-school novel of psychological realism intercut into an unapologetically spectacular comic book. But Sammy's narrative is nevertheless compelled by the same wrenching tension as his cousin's, that is, the dynamic between escape and engagement. Although his head teems with outrageous tales, Sammy's life is achingly dreary. He is the lifeless man of clay awaiting animation. Indeed in his backstory, we hear how years earlier polio rendered Sammy's legs permanently weakened. That crippled state mirrors Sammy's emotional state. Shy, socially awkward, uninterested in pursuing women and uncertain why the arranged dates he endures leave him so empty, Sammy struggles with questions of his sexual orientation. He has had no strong male influence—his father abandoned the family early on (yet another of Chabon's slick auto-liberationists) to pursue a dead-end career in the dying days of vaudeville as a diminutive muscle-bound strongman known as the Mighty

Molecule. (During one of the father's rare visits, Sammy poignantly begs him to take him along. The father promises but is gone when Sammy wakes up the following morning.) Sammy learns in a letter that his father had been killed in a freak accident, crushed during a show while attempting to upend a tractor—the superhero squashed. Given such an inelegant reality and the thin prospects of ever moving beyond its iron inevitabilities, Sammy is drawn not surprisingly to the compelling elegance and sweet escape of comic-book plotlines. Seeing his cousin's dazzling artwork and fancying himself a savvy entrepreneur, Sammy manages to fast-talk his boss at the novelty factory on the idea of backing a comic book (independent of actually having an idea for one) as a way to help advertise the company's whoopee cushions and midget radios. His boss is intrigued and gives Sammy and Joe a weekend to come up with a concept—the result is the Escapist. Over the next several years, even as the Escapist comics find their audience, Sammy creates the storylines for a variety of other equally fabulous comic book heroes, engaging his inexhaustible imagination to transport him, despite his bent soda-straw legs, to distant galaxies and fantastic metropolises.

But Chabon warns, much as Joe cannot find comfort in the comic books they create, that escape is no solace for his cousin. Even as the comics succeed, the lonely Sammy struggles with private demons (unlike his cousin with his broad campaign against the demons of history). The same night at the same party in which Joe so dramatically rescues the choking Dalí and first introduces himself to Rosa, Sammy undergoes his own remarkable, if far more understated epiphany. Wandering alone in the mansion's backrooms, he happens to see in a darkened pantry two men fervently, lovingly caressing and kissing, their elaborate mustaches entangled. It is his first exposure to the reality of homosexual contact—not some furtive back alley assignation that he had long imagined but rather "kissing the way people kissed in the movies, with care and vigor and just a hint of showiness" (254). He bolts from the party, convincing himself that the beautiful kiss had been a hallucination and resigning himself once again to a life of loneliness. It is only later when he visits the radio studio where the Escapist will be broadcast as a serial that he comes under the heady spell of a gorgeous radio actor, Tracy Bacon, hired to play the Escapist. He is enthralled by the "audible brilliance" of the actor's "fifty amp smile" (501). Sammy has his bat-to-the-head moment when his carefully constructed fantasy becomes real—this faux-Escapist can really free him. Days later, just after midnight, Sammy diligently mans the observation deck of the Empire State Building as part of the civilian patrol engaged to watch the horizon for enemy aircraft. Tracy Bacon surprises him with shopping bags teeming with wine and exotic food (quail and oysters). And even as a thunderstorm breaks along the horizon, by the hard shine of a powerful bolt of lightning, the two kiss. In an even more dramatic setting, the two later consummate their love in the underbelly of the magnificent Perisphere built for the World's Fair, Sammy "listening to the fabulous clockwork of their hearts and lungs, and loving each other" (380). But Chabon here cannot tender the sweet redemption of Grady Tripp's love—the burgeoning affair between Sammy and the radio actor implodes when the two are caught in bed during a raid orchestrated by sympathizers of the same pro-German organization whose offices Joe had vandalized. Sammy avoids prosecution only by servicing one of the federal agents who conduct the raid. Debased and humiliated, Sammy is filled with regret and fear—he contemplates going off to California with his lover but panics over the danger, the shame, the risk. "I don't want to be like this," he decides (420). Later he finds out that Tracy Bacon has been killed overseas, an airman in the Pacific theater.

When his cousin Joe departs to join the Navy, Sammy heroically assumes responsibility for Rosa's pregnancy. He marries her, more than willing (unlike Richard Case) to raise another man's son. And after the war, while Joe maintains his seclusion, amid the boom of post-war America, amid the economic security and comfort of the new suburbia, Sammy is still a misfit. He is devastated by poor investments and, ten years after the war when his eccentric cousin suddenly reenters his life, Sammy is grinding out low-end pulp comics and stoically attending to the commonplace sacrifices of household duties. He maintains the difficult pretense of husband and father and is terrified by the implications of someone revealing his secret nightlife of cruising. Even as Joe reunites with Rosa and his biological son (Sammy uses his "connections" with a gay detective to secure Joe's release after he is arrested for the Empire State Building prank), Sammy understands that the difficult masquerade of his life must now end. Although Joe offers to use his considerable savings to bankroll Sammy's dream of owning a comic-book business, Sammy understands that he has no place there any longer.

Hard on the heels of a lawsuit settlement in which the Escapist character is officially retired (it is judged to be too close to the copyrighted Superman), Sammy makes the most heroic gesture in Chabon's comic-book narrative: he will give up the "never-more-than-theoretical family" he had so diligently maintained for the ten years that his cousin had pulled a Wakefield (656). When a government subcommittee probing connections between comic books and teenage delinquency subpoenas Sammy and its chair compels him to admit his homosexuality on live television, Sammy is actually relieved.

He understands, as his cousin came to understand, that he can no longer sustain his auto-liberation, his own coaxing and seductive retreat, that his decade-long imprisonment as a suburban husband and father is as much a Wakefield escape as his cousin's entombment in his Empire State Building bunker. Sammy says goodbye to his family. (The boy he has raised as his son recoils from him, clearly uncomfortable with any intimate contact given his father's electrifying revelation that day on television.) He quietly departs for California to find work in television, to produce, rather than live, within illusions.

And there Chabon closes his narrative. The earnest Joe is poised on the difficult work of rebuilding a traumatized family that he had shattered by his own selfishness. And the stoic Sammy goes off to pursue the slim hope of contentment far away from the only family, indeed the only life, he has ever known, ready now to be just what he is, a gifted if unemployed gay writer. We are given two Wakefields hesitatingly crossing uncertain thresholds. Like Hawthorne, Chabon is unwilling or unable to chart that difficult reentry. Unlike *Wonder Boys,* we are not offered the tailor-fit of a tidy happy ending. We are left one coda shy of Grady Tripp's luminous ending, left with questions rather than resolutions. And that courageous close is in the end the keenest measure of Chabon's maturation. As with the unsettling short stories that Chabon completed even as he worked out the argument of *Kavalier & Clay,* we must adjust to the difficult consolation and deliberate insufficiency of "perhaps." Will the ordinary sustain? Perhaps. We recall that when Joe must rescue a distressed Salvador Dalí when his elaborate diving suit malfunctions, how, once rescued, the flamboyant artist gratefully gulps the welcome salvation of ordinary air. Chabon's point, of course, is that it is not the artist's function to pretend away the complex simplicities of the ordinary. Chabon concedes that narrative cannot fix the world, cannot protect the vulnerable, the terrified, the threatened. Recall the magical Golem, a construct of enormous effort and invention, that for centuries was believed to come to life whenever the Jewish population of Prague was in danger. Years after he is secreted out of occupied Prague in the packing-crate coffin designed to carry the Golem to safety, Joe finally tracks down the crate. When he opens it, he finds no Golem inside, only a soggy pile of river dirt, scum, and ashes.

Chabon argues that art cannot console, cannot protect with happy endings and tidy resolutions. The imagination is like the Golem itself, the "expression of a yearning that a few magic words and an artful hand might produce something—one poor, dumb, powerful thing—exempt from the crushing strictures, from the ills, cruelties and inevitable failures of the greater

Creation" (582). For Chabon, who is now entering the prime of his career, that yearning is the only benediction the writer can tender.[5] Indeed the advice given by the Czech master magician who teaches Josef Kavalier the art of auto-liberation might well summarize Chabon's endorsement of the difficult work of engaging rather than escaping reality: "Never worry about what you are escaping *from*. . . . Reserve your anxieties for what you are escaping *to*" (57).

CHAPTER 6

Summerland and *The Yiddish Policemen's Union*

Negotiate the unpredictable urgencies of the here and now. It was certainly a brave, even heroic, proposition. But "here" and "now" had long been a problematic geography for Chabon, such apparently iron parameters always blurred within his vision. Indeed within Chabon's vision, here and now had long sported quotation marks to indicate their indeterminacy, their elusiveness, their slippery inaccessibility. At best the "here" and "now," for Chabon, were fluid and open, at worst disappointing, insufficient, even claustrophobic. After all, shattered early on by his parents' divorce, Chabon long struggled to find roots, never really trusting in any here or in any now to abide the expectations of stability, reliability, or sturdiness. Long before he determined that he could craft invented worlds for a living, Chabon had regularly—and happily—escaped into fabulous unreal estate, magic kingdoms, and protective sanctuaries. After all he grew up in an essentially imaginary town, an experimental community-of-the-future, a model world that existed at the time largely on paper, its neat and tidy geometric grid of streets only theoretical. He happily spent nights wandering about the fey landscapes of Disney's Florida theme park, poring over the park's souvenir maps by the shaky glare of a pocket flashlight, his bedclothes tented to enclose him entirely in those model worlds he was animating. As a teen Chabon eagerly retreated into the colorful worlds of comic-book panels, this afternoon a fabulous distant planet, tomorrow some shadowy metropolis. An ardent Trekkie, Chabon happily accompanied the starship *Enterprise* and Captain Kirk out into the final frontier, those vast star-chart territories, strange new worlds, new civilizations animated within the narrow frame of his color television. (By thirteen

Chabon spoke fluent Klingon.) And more sobering, he was raised as part of the first generation of Jewish Americans born entirely after the Holocaust and thus grappling with the horror of such genocide primarily as a construction of words, as either an event detailed in books or as vivid testimony from survivors. Chabon grew up aware that Jewish identity in the post-Holocaust world hinged on the fate of the state of Israel, a kind of political and military magic kingdom in its own right, an ever-threatened manifestation of bold, visionary words, a model world declared into existence by international agreement.

Because here and now had long been fragile, vulnerable constructs for Chabon, his two follow-up works to *Kavalier & Clay* would continue his fascination with the complex dynamic between the centripetal pull of the imagination and the centrifugal push of the immediate. Now he was prepared, however, to offer a most sweeping apologia for the imagination. As texts the two works took breathtaking risks. *Summerland* (2002) is a free-ranging Harry Potter-Frodo Baggins-styled young adult fantasy set in an alternative universe that plays host to a titanic, (literally) apocalyptic baseball game. *The Yiddish Policemen's Union* (2007) is a haunting noir murder mystery/alternative-history fantasy set in a fictitious Jewish refugee state established after World War II by the American government in the forbidding islands of the Alaskan panhandle. Veteran readers of Chabon were not surprised. Surely the achievement of *Kavalier & Clay,* its clarion call to animate the heroic counterforce of the here and now and to engage that world, eyes unblinking and full of light, rather than surrender to the seductive escape of the imagination, could never stand as Chabon's final word. These two follow-up works indeed marked a complicated take on this career-long fascination with the dynamic between the imaginary and the real. Chabon now offered two bold, gaudy works that ultimately take place not between the characters, or between the characters and the reader, but rather within the subtle dynamic between Chabon and the reader. Recall Chabon's wistful valedictory to the imagination in *Kavalier & Clay* and its inability to produce a substantive something against the press of history and circumstance, some "poor, dumb thing—exempt from the failures of greater Creation" (592). Liberated into newfound confidence, Pulitzer in hand, positioned now among the most promising voices of the post-Pynchon era, Chabon was ready to fashion just exactly that poor, dumb thing.

Although the theme was certainly familiar, it appeared that the treatment of the theme in these two works marked a major departure for Chabon. Few contemporary writers of serious fiction had ever risked such an apparently drastic break with their signature fictional template. For readers only familiar with Chabon's Pulitzer Prize–winning historic epic, these two books would appear to mark an inexplicable rupture in Chabon's narrative development. They accompanied a series of quarterly comic books that Chabon published, featuring some of the superhero figures from *Kavalier & Clay*, and the slender novella *The Final Solution* (2004), published in *The Paris Review* and recipient of the magazine's prestigious Aga Khan Prize for Fiction. The novella's aging, pipe-puffing detective, presumably Sherlock Holmes (the subject of Chabon's first short story back in grade school), comes out of retirement during World War II to help solve a baroque murder mystery that involves a garrulous parrot. The bird's apparently nonsense utterances actually reveal the account numbers of Nazi Swiss bank accounts set up to launder monies stolen from Jews consigned to the concentration camps. These narratives were so obviously and unapologetically unreal that they appeared to mark a radical break into new and decidedly offbeat directions. They represent a kind of wacky, albeit splendid, midlife crisis for Chabon, then in his early forties. He seemed bent on abandoning his long commitment to serious fiction. Given the sheer weight of the *Kavalier & Clay* project (recall his disastrous attempt at such epic scale a decade earlier with "Fountain City"), or perhaps because of his new celebrity, or perhaps because of the beckoning call of the marketplace, Chabon seemed intent on producing footnote works, fun books, entertainments executed solely with the light-speed whimsy of a dilettante. Chabon trades his harrowing excavations into the Holocaust, mercenary capitalism, and the ugly logic of homophobia for the unironic excess of harmless and engaging stories, a well-earned hiatus while we all awaited his return to the serious business of serious fiction.[1]

This so-called midlife crisis, however, would last more than a decade, really until the appearance in late 2012 of *Telegraph Avenue*. It would produce some of Chabon's most remarkable and accomplished fictions. Clearly far more was going on than some odd side-excursions into campy marketplace genres. Veteran readers recognized in the giddy embrace of such a loopy range of genres, in the sheer imaginative excesses of both *Summerland* and *The Yiddish Policemen's Union*, a manifestation of Chabon's abiding fascination with the energy of the imagination to offer shelter, a place both a part and apart. Despite the works' plethora of vividly realized characters, the dominant character in both fantasy works is undoubtedly place: the four vast alternate worlds through which young Ethan Feld must journey and the forbidding, frozen world of the Alaskan Jewish state. In both cases, Chabon boldly animates entirely original worlds, places that are at once nowhere and now-here.

Far from some flighty hiatus from the serious business of serious fiction, Chabon tests the premise he had proposed as early as the summer of Art

Bechstein's maturation. If the imagination cannot undo catastrophe, cannot redeem history from its brutalities; if the imagination cannot reshape raw event into meaning and gift the dirty dishwater of everyday reality with radiance; if the imagination ultimately cannot script the fractal confusions of the immediate into meaningful pattern; if the imagination cannot alchemically convert the lead of everyday things into the handy gold of meaningful symbols; if the imagination cannot finally redeem the disappointments, frustrations, casual hopes and tiny joys, the deep expectations of circumstance within the prison house of contingency, surely it can nevertheless produce something audacious, something robust, something necessary, and, yes, something significant.

Against the powerful pull of the larger cultural addictions to the easy accessibility of film and television, video games and the Internet, Chabon in these defining mid-career works heroically repositions narrative itself. He dares to challenge a generation's imagination, stunted by the oppressive thereness and dreary accessibility of the visual media, to rediscover what Chabon had discovered as a child: the reassuring immediacy of unreal estate. Despite vast differences in their dilemmas, the Little League hero Ethan Feld and the burned-out detective Meyer Landsman both exist within fabulous texts, marvelous somethings. Their narratives are defiant expressions of a resilient imagination, the fabulous reach of invention, a manifestation of the very energy that Art Bechstein so casually abuses, that Grady Tripp too quickly rejects, that Nathan Shapiro comes to disdain and distrust even as he acquiesces to gherkins in his tuna salad, and that Sammy Clay only reluctantly abandons to engage the ordinary world. Perhaps as a kind of rescue first-response to the deep trauma of September 11th, Chabon, in the troubled opening decade of the twenty-first century, ministers to a culture in crisis. Born exiles in an inhospitable post-postmodern world of excess and brutality, Chabon's reader here is catapulted beyond the now—facticity, history, memory—and into the fabulous. At mid-career Chabon offers his reader nothing less than a real home in an unreal place. It is temporary, certainly, but it is a place from which we will return refreshed, reinvigorated, empowered to do what Chabon's characters to date had never quite pulled off: balancing the delight in the imagination with the obligations of the real.

The curious epigraph to *The Yiddish Policemen's Union* surely underscores this evolution in Chabon's argument. It is taken from "The Jumblies," a wonderful mock epic by the irreverent Victorian nonsense poet Edward Lear. The poem tells of a courageous and patently absurd handful of Jumblies who dare to set out to explore the vast ocean in a simple flimsy sieve-boat. Certain they will be lost at sea, their ever pragmatic and drearily clear-sighted friends beg them not to launch, pointing out the evident absurdity of trying to float in such an obviously vulnerable craft. The friends—and surely Lear's more pragmatic readers—are stunned to find at poem's end that the Jumblies' voyage has lasted more than twenty years, and that, in that time, they had seen much of the wide and wonderful world. Such is the unsuspected sturdiness, Chabon suggests, of the imagination itself. He offers the reader a most captivating adventure if we are willing to trust to its flimsy sturdiness. Chabon dares the reader to accept the thing in hand, a book, the equivalent of the sieve-boat. It is, he cautions, a created thing that offers a clear parameter, a portal into the boundless geography of the audacious and the fantastic, a world conjured by the writer but animated by the reader, a text-world we visit rather than inhabit. These two landmark works function much like the sumptuous theme parks Chabon so loved as a boy. They are magic kingdoms from which the reader/visitor returns restored, reanimated, Chabon re-aligning his fiction to explore the dynamic between reader and writer, a measure of a writer hardly taking some quirky sabbatical.

Surely the most daring expression of Chabon's post-*Kavalier* investigation into the robust realities of the imagination would have to be the unapologetically brash, unironically sprawling fantasy adventure *Summerland,* among the most audacious works of American sports fiction in the last quarter century. Hard on the heels of the Pulitzer Prize–winning *Kavalier,* with its documentarian realism, its sobering investigations into the evils of religious bigotry and homophobia, and its period-accurate setting, the plot-rich narrative of *Summerland* recounts a fabulous baseball game in an alternative world, which decides the fate of the cosmos itself. A showdown is played out almost entirely by fabulous creatures, among them a friendly giant, a menacing goblin, a diabolic overlord, an enchanted princess, a thieving giant rat, and even a nine-foot, two-centuries old pet Sasquatch. Its multiple baroque plotlines would certainly make extraordinary demands on young readers for whom, remarkably enough, the novel was originally marketed. (Chabon dedicated the book to his own children, often telling interviewers he had wanted, at last, to write a book his kids could enjoy.) The lavish work drew enthusiastic comparisons to the ambitious imaginative richness of iconic fantasy writers such as J. R. R. Tolkien and J. K. Rowling. *Summerland* became one of the year's best-selling young-adult titles, and was listed by the *New York Times* among that genre's year-end best-of titles. It was awarded the prestigious Mythopoeic Award that recognizes the finest work of fantasy for young-adult readers. And it was later optioned, appropriately by Disney, to be developed into a major animation project.

But much like *The Wizard of Oz,* the classic 1939 MGM film that clearly influences Chabon's vision here (as it had so often before), *Summerland* offers much to an adult perception. Like the MGM film, *Summerland* begins modestly in a kind of austere black-and-white realism. We start within a conventional coming-of-age sports narrative, a time-tested genre in which a socially maladjusted if hypersensitive child must mature amid the challenge of testing athletic skills that he initially resists or simply ignores. The story moves toward a competition that demands both courage and skill but also expands the child's narrow moral and emotional horizons. He ultimately develops a sturdy sense of self-identity that promises a confident entrance into adulthood. Eleven-year-old Ethan Feld, a nerdy kid with a precocious vocabulary and a fondness for educational television, lives on remote Clam Island in Puget Sound in the Pacific Northwest. (We are provided with a meticulously detailed hand-drawn map of the island). His father, a brilliant if eccentric retired aeronautical engineer, works in a garage lab to develop a private dirigible that could someday replace the family car. Among the island kids, Ethan struggles to fit in. He and his father have only recently moved to the island from Colorado after his vibrant mother, a gifted veterinarian, died after a long struggle with cancer. Ethan feels emotionally estranged from his father. The two are unable to share the lacerating grief they both feel, and each retreats into awkward isolation.

At the insistence of his father (a crackerjack southpaw pitcher back in the day who had dreamed of playing professional baseball), Ethan dutifully plays centerfield for Ruth's Fluff 'n' Fold Roosters in the local Mustang League. The problem is that Ethan lacks any recognizable talent. He finds the nine-inning grind tedious, his mind unavailable to the game's subtle tactical moves. He is prone to reverie and regularly commits egregious fielding errors, and he laments that the game actually keeps track of errors. Anytime he approaches the plate to bat, even his most stalwart friend on the team, the far more gifted Jennifer T. Rideout, a fellow misfit in a troublingly dysfunctional family, recognizes the inevitability of the strikeout. Indeed the team, which has a lopsided losing record, only threatens to win in games when Ethan rides the bench. His teammates taunt him, they beg the coach to bench him, within his earshot they carp about his abundant shortcomings. As the narrative opens and as they drive to that evening's game, Ethan begs his father to let him quit. But Ethan is stuck. Baseball is not only part of his father's upbringing, it is as well a cherished element of life on Clam Island. Local folklore holds that the endless dreary rains that soak the island never fall on Summerland, the island's impeccably manicured baseball field.

We are in the familiar, dingy realism of a conventional sports-fiction landscape. We have the misfit, an athletically challenged geek, indifferent to the implications of sports and immune to the adrenaline rush of competition, keen to abandon the field of someone else's dreams and return to the cozy protected environment of his own bedroom. Ethan is a brainiac trying to live up to the (un)real expectations of a lost-jock parent determined that his unfulfilled dreams of athletic glory might, at last, be achieved by his offspring.[2] We are ready for one of two inevitable endings: either the boy will learn the value of sports and reveal unsuspected talent or the father will learn to make a difficult peace with what his son is. Along the way both father and son may learn any one of a number of sports power clichés: Be True to Yourself; Be Honest with Those You Love; Recognize Your Talents; Do Your Best; Winners Never Quit, Quitters Never Win; Work Hard and Rewards Will Follow, etc.

But such conventional narration is manifestly not what Chabon is about. For all the careful details of life on Clam Island, it is unlike Baum's dreary rural Kansas. Despite the handy map of the island and Chabon's deft re-creation of the island's specifics—its drizzly weather; its eccentric citizenry; its rich history (including the catastrophic collapse in 1943 of the only bridge that connected the island to the mainland); its unspoiled woodland interior (now threatened by mercenary developers); its patchwork grid of gravel backroads; its rustic stores and run-down hotels and century-old ramshackle homes—Clam Island is entirely fictitious, a magic kingdom that exists only on paper, conjured entirely by Chabon, his own private Columbia. That fact alone is not shattering in its implications (countless writers have created fictitious settings as backdrops for otherwise realistic storylines). But for veteran readers of Chabon, *Summerland* marks the first time Chabon moved so dramatically, so entirely into unreal estate, far afield from his usual settings—the blue-collar neighborhoods of Pittsburgh, the environs of suburban Washington, the sun-swept streets of Los Angeles, or the meticulously re-created urban scenes of mid-century Manhattan that Chabon had drawn so carefully and so faithfully from archival research. Here we delight in the convincing reality of an entirely fictitious place, a place that is at once nowhere and now-here.

But Chabon is not content with such modest invention. Within fifty pages, he upends any lingering expectation of tidy realism and vaults his coming-of-age sports narrative into a most unexpected dimension. As Ethan perfunctorily mans centerfield, the boy grows increasingly bored and impulsively heads into the nearby woods in the hopes of seeing a strange fox-like creature he and his father had glimpsed from the car on the way to the field. In short order Ethan is introduced to a half-blind little man who is missing a finger and sporting a ragged ponytail. He identifies himself as Chiron "Ringfinger" Brown, a baseball scout from the old Negro Leagues, a fellow who apparently can read minds and is invisible to everyone else. The apparition speaks to Ethan cryptically about his current scouting mission: to find a hero, presumably Ethan himself. Bewildered Ethan returns to the game. But strange things are suddenly afoot. For the first time in the island residents' memory, rain falls on the emerald greens of Summerland and abruptly shortens the game. The following morning Ethan awakens to find the strange little animal he had glimpsed from the car now straddling his chest, calmly smoking a pipe cut from bone. He is Cutbelly, an 800-year-old fox-monkey, an emissary from a parallel universe peopled by diminutive fairies known as ferishers.

Much as in *The Wizard of Oz*, in which we quick-cut from the chiaroscuro half-light of Kansas to the liberating colors of Munchkinland, here Cutbelly escorts the boy (and us) to that alternate universe even as he explains to Ethan the dire dilemma the world faces. A master-fiend known only as Coyote has determined, after unendurable millennia, that it is time to destroy creation itself, made up of four complementary worlds of which Earth, or the Middling, is but one. Coyote is determined to poison the Murmury Well, a pool of water no wider than a country pond but "deeper than sleep" that feeds the great Tree of Worlds, which alone provides the four worlds their superstructure.[3] That rapidly approaching apocalyptic moment has been dubbed Ragged Rock. (This is perhaps a corruption of "Ragnarök," a harrowing event recounted in Norse mythology when the sun is devoured by a wolf and the earth submerged in water.[4]) An oracle in the ferisher world, a giant clam named Johnny Speakwater, has confirmed Ethan's improbable status as the Middling's savior, the one who must stop Coyote. In case the stunned young boy doubts his calling, when a sinister raven (perhaps the master shape-changer Coyote himself) suddenly swoops down and carries off the helpless oracle, Ethan takes a smooth round (baseball-like) rock and in one careful throw beans the disappearing crow. The crow drops the clam, which strikes Ethan on the head, knocking him out cold.

He awakens back home, certain that no one would believe his story. In short order, however, he confides in Jennifer T. Rideout and finds that her great aunts and her uncle, members of the Salishan, a dwindling Native American tribe indigenous to the island, not only know about Coyote but know the danger he poses. And when Ethan discovers that the Coyote's minions have abducted his father (Coyote wants to use the picoderm, the resilient polymer that the father has invented for his prototype dirigible, as the delivery system for the poison), Ethan is determined to cross over into the alternate universe where Coyote dwells. Using ferisher magic, Ethan redesigns the family's gaudy orange Saab station wagon into a working airship, and with Jennifer and another misfit classmate, the nerdy Thor Wignutt, who is convinced that he is actually an android, Ethan sets out on a journey to rescue his father and save the universe. We have traveled from the reassuring realism of the opening chapters into a fetching, freewheeling over-the-rainbow fantasy that never pretends to be anything but a gorgeous, vivid playscape. It is a sort of *Bad News Bears* meets *The Wizard of Oz,* Chabon delighting in the play of sheer invention as Ethan journeys across multiple worlds toward his inevitable showdown with Coyote. As it turns out, Thor is actually a shadowtail, a genetic changeling that is part human and part ferisher with sufficient magic to enable him to guide them all between the worlds. And so Ethan's grand adventure begins.

As Ethan journeys to save the world and his father, he gathers about him, one by one, a ragtag gang of misfits that becomes his crew and ultimately his baseball team, a narrative strategy that of course recalls Dorothy and her gathering-in along the Yellow Brick Road. When, a malicious giant named Mooseknuckle John snags the flying Saab in his furry hand, he threatens to eat the kids but agrees gamely to a wager. If Ethan can catch three of his blazing pitches, he will let them all go on their way. As Ethan prepares for the showdown (he has never been a catcher, he had always been exiled to the outfield where he could do little harm), Jennifer befriends the giant's pet, a mammoth Sasquatch named Taffy (lovingly detailed by Chabon with the meticulous care of a zoologist), whom the giant had captured two centuries earlier and who grieves the separation from her two children. While Ethan bears down and (with advice from an ancient book of enchantment) successfully catches the three fireball pitches, Jennifer deftly frees the caged Sasquatch (she uses herself as a key). The beast then joins them in their quest. Later when the kids are captured by a menacing band of lady ferishers who bring down the airship with arrows, they are imprisoned with Spider Rose, a feisty, red-haired princess incarcerated for helping Coyote in one of his more nefarious schemes (introducing the designated hitter into baseball) on the promise of being given a baby brother to love. Of course Coyote had tricked the naïve girl and gave her only a most grotesque baby doll, which she drags about with her even now. When Ethan secures their freedom from the prison cell, Spider Rose (and her creepy doll) joins the gang. To ensure their continued passage, Ethan and his friends must later defeat a team of giants, albeit shrinking giants, in a dramatic baseball game. One of the giants, Grim, joins the kids in the end. Add to that a sneaky little were-rat thief named Dick

Pettipaw and, after returning to Ethan's world long enough to secure a ringer, an aging long-ball hitter named Rodrigo Buendía, now relegated to the ignominy of being a designated hitter with the California Angels, and Ethan's crew is complete.

Through it all Ethan helplessly monitors the disintegration of his kidnapped father. Magic glasses allow him to observe his father even as Dr. Feld falls under the enticements of the Mephistophelean Coyote. Ethan grows alarmed as his father wears away while slaving to create the polymer sample in Coyote's lab. (Dr. Feld flattens into a sorry two-dimensional cutout.) And even as his father, long his hero figure, begins literally to thin, even as the journey unfolds, Ethan begins the evolution that recalls Dorothy in *The Wizard of Oz*. Like Dorothy, he tests unsuspected reserves of courage, resourcefulness, and determination. Like Dorothy, he opens up to the dilemma of others (his "team") and to the logic of sacrifice and the vital necessity of teamwork. Like Dorothy who gradually perceives the depth of her aunt and uncle's love for her, Ethan comes to appreciate the magnitude of his father's love for him. Like Dorothy, he shoulders the responsibility of leadership, coming to make critical decisions under enormous pressures. Chabon suggests that maturation symbolically by Ethan's association with a gnarled limb that had been clipped from the Tree of Worlds, a limb that is refashioned into Ethan's very own bat, a charmed wonder stick that empowers Ethan at last to find his groove at the plate. However, the bat has a knot in its handle that rubs Ethan's hand painfully raw, a reminder of the agony inevitable in the transition from childhood.

When Ethan and his band at last arrive at the Diamond Green by the Tree of Worlds, Ethan is still uncertain about his swing. Desperate to avert the apocalypse and knowing that more than anything else Coyote covets Ethan's wonder bat, Jennifer convinces Coyote to accept the challenge of playing a single winner-take-all game for the bat: if his minions win, Coyote not only gets the magic bat but he can go through with his diabolic plan to end creation itself. But if his team loses, he must abandon his apocalyptic scheme without recriminations. It is only now as Jennifer negotiates that bet that we begin to understand the true dimension of Coyote's threat—what he will deliver into the root system of the Tree of Worlds is a potent liquid form of fermented Nothing left over after Creation millennia ago. Once delivered into the Well, it would quickly dissolve the Tree (and the four worlds) into a drab uniform gray, the universe hissing away into entropic nullity. So the Big Game is set: as with the delightful Crayola simplifications of Dorothy and her gang versus the Wicked Witch of the West and hers, it is nothing less than

Evil versus Good; Dark versus Light; Lies versus Hope; Destruction versus Salvation; Death versus Life.

And as in *The Wizard of Oz,* from the outset it doesn't look rosy for the good guys. Coyote's baseball All Stars are as intimidating as they are scurrilous. And in its valiant barnstorming crusade across three worlds, Ethan's team of misfits stands at a woeful 2–7. But much as we give Dorothy and her motley crew little chance as they engage the witch's forbidding castle with its minions of marching Winkie guards and then cheer as the quartet of improbable heroes liquidates the witch, likewise here we cheer as Ethan's ragged team improbably triumphs. The heroic showdown plays out, in classic baseball fashion, in the bottom of the ninth inning. Ethan comes to the plate, his team down by two with two base runners aboard. Rising above the nagging memories of similar games in which he had failed and rising above the excruciating pain in his hand, Ethan clobbers a towering home run of such magnitude that not only does Coyote forfeit the game but the wild arc of the ball itself actually tears a hole in the sky and releases back in the Middling a flood of enchantment: orphans find their parents; cancers go into remission; dying coral reefs suddenly bloom; in casinos career losers hit the jackpot; and those who mourn the dead are gifted with vivid dreams in which they can communicate at length with the departed. It is the moment of the Unsealing, a healing flood of rejuvenating spirit.

Importantly, much as in *The Wizard of Oz,* with the arch-agent of evil so entirely vanquished, we quickly depart the fantasy world and return to the far more familiar black-and-white world. But that return is now suffused with new appreciation, new animation, a new commitment to its mundane glories. Like Kansas in *Oz*'s final reel, Clam Island now has a different feel in its conclusion. Ethan affects a touching reunion with his father, who has been restored to three dimensions, and together they begin the work of rebuilding their family. The creepy doll that Spider Rose lugs around morphs into a real baby brother for her to love. The Sasquatch Taffy, who loses her foot after it is burned by a single acidic drop of Nothing (she bravely attacks Coyote when he declares a forfeit in violation of their agreement), is outfitted by a compassionate vet with a prosthetic device made of Dr. Feld's resilient polymer. And in the last pages, we return to the Mustang League, to the very baseball field where we had begun, the field where Ethan had long suffered, bored and unengaged. Ethan's team, long the joke of the league, has staged a miraculous late-season surge and finds itself in a one-game playoff for the championship. Now the team's catcher, Ethan makes the game's big play by holding onto a ball despite a fierce collision with a careening base runner intent on scoring. We close the book with this grand heroic moment: "When [Ethan] stood up again, his mouth was full of dirt, he had taken a knee in the eye, and his nose was bleeding. But he was still holding on to the ball" (500). Like Dorothy Gale, Ethan has learned there really is no place like home. He is at last at peace, a modest hero at home in a modest black-and-white world.

But Chabon is about more than an elaborate homage to *The Wizard of Oz*. With all its fabulous razzle-dazzle, *Summerland* is, unlike the MGM film, a told tale, a frame narrative with a voiceover that regularly breaks into the action, an "I" that invariably calls attention to the toldness of the tale. Chabon, or a Chabon surrogate, tells us the story, swearing all along to its authenticity. Imagine if auteur film director Victor Fleming had periodically leaned over the camera lens, right into the movie's frame, and had spoken directly to audiences, recalling how tricky the camera shots were when they were actually filming over the rainbow in the real Munchkinland. In *Summerland* we are never allowed to ease into the coaxing enchantment of Chabon's other world fantasy—Chabon periodically interrupts the action to reassert his presence, a geek (he describes himself as a "big, ungainly adult" [429]) who pores over baseball stats and box scores. He is fascinated as much by recounting the fabulous quest toward the showdown game, which he does with meticulous verisimilitude, as by reviewing the physics of pitching and the math of hitting. With a nerdy fascination for data, he reassures us of the fabulous narrative's reliability. We delight in a fantasy that we are reassured is real, the exertion of the authentic hero of a narrative crowded with hero types: Chabon the storyteller.

Thus as we read, absorbed by the reach of Chabon's creativity, we always know that, unlike Chabon's previous novels, here we are in a constructed space, a place at once real and unreal, a fabulous narrative space offered, like one of Disney's premier theme parks, with sufficient effects to feel real—yet one that is wonderfully, decidedly not. It is a jolting narrative strategy that reassures the reader that the fantastic realm welcomes us whenever we care to "visit." The text is at once apart from and a part of our reality. Reading it is akin to settling down for yet another happy rewind of *Oz,* a safe haven available whenever the reader feels the yen to head over the rainbow. Without condescension or irony, *Summerland* ministers, joyfully and compassionately, to our yearning for a "deep and tiny world" apart, its fabulous narrative a readily available model world as therapeutic and inviting as it is temporary. But this is a narrative of return. Unlike Dorothy Gale, we always know we are three heel clicks away from returning to the here and now. Yet it is the achievement of Chabon's vision that when we return, like Ethan, we return reanimated, revived, ready to undertake with renewed energy the here and the now.

But Chabon understands that "return to" is but the other side of "exile from," so he poses the inevitable question. What if the returning is more difficult, the world more pressing, the threat more menacing, more immediate? What if home is, finally, inaccessible, distant, even lost? What use then is the imagination, even at full throttle? Even as Chabon was completing work on his gorgeous baseball fantasy with its upbeat endorsement of the rhythm of retreat and return, he had begun to investigate the question inevitably raised by such a reassuring narrative. He developed a kind of counter-story, this one more for adults, that would test the darker implications of the centripetal reach of the imagination by positioning the same sort of audacious text-shelter—that is, a narrative that launches off into a most fabulous and entirely unreal place—amid a far more threatening real world. This world would not be dominated by some testy, shape-changing malevolent demi-god who had for millennia brooded over obliterating the cosmos by literally poisoning the wellspring of creation. Chabon instead decides to test the tensile strength of a narrative-shelter by positioning it against the hard reality of virulent, centuries-old anti-Semitism.

The idea for what would become his ambitious novel *The Yiddish Policemen's Union* (2007) began germinating nearly a decade earlier. Wandering about a California bookstore, Chabon chanced upon an out-of-print pocket-sized travelers' Yiddish phrasebook. He was intrigued to imagine, given the rapidly decreasing number of speakers of the language, a place where Yiddish would still be the dominant language. Within the splendid reach of "what if," Chabon with ingenious daring challenged the imagination to reshape history itself to accommodate such a place. Imagine a contemporary world without the nation-state of Israel. What if months before the attack on Pearl Harbor in 1940 when America was still officially neutral, Chabon posits, Congress acted in concert with the Roosevelt Administration and backed the Slattery Report? This visionary document produced by the Department of the Interior recommended opening the Alaskan wilderness to Jewish refugees from Europe as both a haven for them from the aggressive brutality of Hitler and as a pragmatic strategy to help develop the largely unsettled territory. And what if the sole Alaskan politician who was fearful of a long-term Jewish takeover of the territory, the figure in fact most responsible for blocking the vote and thus single-handedly dooming the idea, what if rather than blocking the bill he had died unexpectedly, say, in a car accident? Chabon asks us to imagine the American Northwest suddenly opened up and millions of oppressed European Jews, facing the menace of Nazi brutality accepting the offer of asylum in a distant and decidedly hostile frontier much like first-generation Puritans.

But Chabon was far from finished. Imagine three years after the war, say, an attempted state of Israel in the Holy Land is obliterated in a bloody conflict with the combined military of the region's Arab populations, a war that reduces Palestine to a tangled, violent chaos of conflicting religious and political interests and Jerusalem itself to a "city of blood and slogans painted on the wall, severed heads on telephone poles."[5] Imagine that the American government, haunted by the grim evidence of the Holocaust, quickly agreed to extend the lease on the Alaskan settlement for the Jewish immigrants but only for sixty years because of lingering concerns over a Jewish takeover of the mineral-rich territory. Then imagine, Chabon asks, that amid such an intimidating frozen wasteland, the hardy transplanted Jewry had against all odds actually created a bustling 1500 square mile provisional Jewish state in the archipelago around Sitka, taking root amid the Native American culture of the indigenous Tlingit tribe, and, despite that conflict, had developed Sitka into a major international Yiddish-speaking metropolis, more than five million strong (even hosting a successful World's Fair in 1977). In conjuring this model world, Chabon along the way could undo some of the darkest (and most familiar) episodes of mid-century history: the Holocaust never happened; more than four million Jewish immigrants escaped the Nazi wrath and remained alive; the bombings of Hiroshima and Nagasaki never happened, rather they were replaced by a single, limited strategic atomic bombing of Berlin to end the war quickly; the Vietnam War was never fought, rather a far less insidious, far more contained Monroe Doctrine-style war involving Cuba secured the hemisphere's safety; John F. Kennedy survived his presidency and, still an eligible bachelor, married sultry actress Marilyn Monroe, who never committed suicide; and post-war Russia never cohered long enough to achieve sufficient superpower status to sustain a Cold War.

It is a most convincing alternative reality that, unlike the fabulous dimensions of the multiple fantasy worlds of *Summerland*, is both immediate and believable. *The Yiddish Policemen's Union* takes place in late 2007 in the frantic closing weeks before the Reversion, the date when the American government will reassert possession of the Sitka panhandle and the hardy second-generation Jewish settlers, still without green cards, will once again face the fast approach of yet another wrenching Diaspora, the hard toss into uncertain exile. Unlike *Summerland*, which begins as clear-eyed realism and then catapults into dazzling fantasy, here we begin (and stay) within the unsettling chiaroscuro of realism, a kind of over-the-rainbow *Maltese Falcon*.

In the opening pages we meet Meyer Landsman, a gruff old-school detective straight out of the pages of Dashiell Hammett or Elmore Leonard. He is an ever-rumpled, plain-spoken loner with a signature porkpie hat and a shirttail always hanging out. Perpetually hungover from downing slivovitz from his collection of well-smudged World's Fair shot glasses, he remains mired in a graceless middle-age. Meyer is a realist despite living in the world's largest theocratic state. He savagely mocks the gentle consolations of religion—"heaven is kitsch, God a word, and the soul, at most, the charge on your battery" (130). But he is also a hard-core romantic, divorced for two years but still carrying a torch for his sultry, sassy ex-wife, Bina. The talented, rogue homicide detective is now so burned out that he fantasizes about taking his service revolver and carefully, surgically blowing off his head. He bears the immense weight of a difficult and shadowy past with heavy-hearted Hemingwayesque grace: his father was driven to suicide over the guilt of having been among the survivors of the Nazi camps. Three years earlier, after fifteen years of trying to have children, he and his wife reluctantly decided to abort their baby exactly seventeen weeks and one day into the pregnancy after a grim prognosis of possible genetic abnormalities; and just months earlier his free-spirited kid sister, a licensed bush pilot, had died in a mysterious plane crash in the rugged islands off Sitka.

We meet Landsman, his life and career in free fall, living month to month in a rundown flophouse in one of Sitka's seedier neighborhoods. In the opening pages, Landsman is rousted by the hotel's manager. In a room three floors below Landsman, a young drifter, a heroin addict, is discovered dead, a single shot to the back of the head. With the honed instincts of more than twenty years on the force, Landsman is immediately intrigued—as much by the half-finished game of chess the dead man left behind, which seems freighted with significance (Landsman discovers that the young man was an accomplished chess prodigy), as by the deliberate execution-style shooting, an extravagance for such an apparently unimportant junkie. Ever the maverick, he pursues the case because his new supervisor, who happens to be the very ex-wife for whom he still pines, expressively forbids anyone in the department from investigating the killing of such an unimportant lowlife. (The department is concerned over leaving outstanding cases when the bureau must close when the territory is returned to Alaskan control in a handful of weeks.) But mostly, as Landsman admits, he has never much liked puzzles—and so we are off. Much as when Ethan shadowtails off with Cutbelly and we are introduced, wide-eyed, to Chabon's fabulous world, here we are quickly, easily hooked. Chabon creates the irresistible gravitational pull of a stylish murder mystery and a deft reanimation of the familiar character dynamics from a generation of detective-noir classics. He delivers syllable-crisp, pitch-perfect rendering of the genre's crackling repartee dialogue as well as the extravagant sense of simile and Leonardesque clipped sentences. But perhaps what most engages here, as in *Summerland,* is Chabon's evocation of place, the meticulous care with which he reconstructs the entirely fabulous world of the makeshift Jewish state of Sitka—its harsh weather, labyrinthine mean streets, eccentric residents, peculiar music and food, and even its language (a delightful registry of Yiddish neologisms for which Chabon provides a glossary).[6] To borrow the premise of *The Wizard of Oz* that so dominated *Summerland*, it's as if Chabon re-creates the fabulous nowhere of Oz in the careful verisimilitude and documentarian blacks and whites of Kansas. In short, the un-real becomes a most fetching real.

Although a newcomer to the genre, Chabon stage-manages the murder mystery with a deft confidence. Landsman begins the hard-core gumshoe work of investigating the shooting assisted by his partner (and cousin), the half-Tlingit, half-Jewish Berko Shemets, whose stable and loving domestic life casts Landsman's sad and solitary lifestyle in stark relief. Landsman discovers the victim is one Mendel Shpilman, a former chess prodigy and the estranged only son of a formidable Hasidic rabbi. Shpilman's father is the reputed leader of a radical conservative sect called the Verbovers, a Mafia-like syndicate known by its square black hats that controls the streets of Sitka with a crude combination of faith and intolerance. They enforce an uncompromising piety and unyielding morality with ruthless and brutal efficiency against those perceived to be the theocratic settlement's infidels, "beings so flawed, corrupted, and hopeless of redemption that only cosmic courtesy led the Verbovers even to consider them human at all" (99). When Landsman meets the notorious rabbi, he confronts a massive "deformed mountain, a giant ruined desert, a cartoon house with the windows shut and the sink left running" (135). The rabbi in turn tells the detective the bitter history of his doomed son. Like eleven-year old Ethan Feld, who was recruited as a superhero, liberator, and savior, Mendel Shpilman as a child was revered in his neighborhood as his people's savior. (He had a twin brother, born dead, widely interpreted as a sign.) With an IQ of 170, intensely spiritual, and schooled early in Jewish law to become a rabbi, Mendel was reputed to have given off an other-worldly warmth, a physical feeling of comfort and welcome. He was reputed to have even worked miracles, including curing a woman of cancer, while he tangled with the unseemly realities of human behavior, unable to find his way to optimism or hope. Despite his melancholia, Mendel was widely regarded as the Tzaddik Ha-Dor, that one-in-a-generation Messiah figure, a cultural fixture in the two thousand-year narrative of expectation and disappointment long part of the Jewish faith. Here the savior figure, however, unlike the buoyant Ethan Feld, will be driven into existential angst. Distraught over suspicions of his own homosexuality (he visits his mother once in flamboyant drag), Mendel wanted no part of being a messiah, seeking refuge in the dead end of addiction. So for more than twenty years, the father explains, Mendel Shpilman, his son—the street junkie, the lapsed Jew, the deep-in-the-closet gay man—had been dead to him.

Landsman discovers that the tormented Mendel had in the end actually begged a friend to shoot him mercifully and quickly. With its savior figure driven to calculated, desperate self-destruction, *The Yiddish Policemen's Union* functions as a sobering (and necessary) counterargument to the giddiness of *Summerland* and represents a darker, far more brooding adult version of that splendid fantasy. Unlike Ethan Feld and his reprise of Dorothy Gale's heroic return home, the closing here is decidedly muted. In the tradition of classic noir fiction, Landsman becomes entangled in a complicated international geopolitical intrigue. In pursuing what he thinks is a case of black-market slave trafficking, Landsman stumbles on a secret quasi-military installation on the remote (and appropriately named) Peril Island, a short flight from Sitka in the protected Tlingit reservation. He uncovers evidence of a cabal of radical Zionist visionaries—"Yids with schemes" (312). With the clandestine help of the anti-Islamist American government, they have been training agents as part of a mission to blow up Islam's revered Dome of the Rock in the divided city of Jerusalem. They intend to ignite a Jewish uprising that would retake Palestine from the Arabs in advance of, at last, rebuilding the Temple. They hope to restore the kingdom-state promised in the heady visions of the Apocalypse in Revelation and in turn ignite the long-feared Holy War. In its way the plot is as catastrophic as Coyote's scheme to poison the Tree of Worlds. Landsman flies to Peril Island but in the process is taken captive by the same paramilitary outfit and must affect a harrowing escape by tossing a cot, to which he has been handcuffed, through a window. He carefully pieces together what must have happened. Verbover henchmen (directed by the rabbi) escorted Mendel to the island under the guise of helping the junkie turn his life around and overcome his heroin addiction—they tell him the island is a rehab clinic renowned for its work with apparently lost causes. Landsman's own sister piloted the small plane that flew Mendel there. Once Mendel arrives, the paramilitary operation revealed their ambitious plans and how they needed a cleaned-up messiah to give religious (and apocalyptic) status to their terrorist mission. Mendel resisted and tried desperately to arrange a flight off the island, again through Landsman's sister. That flight, Landsman is convinced, was deliberately crashed into a mountain before it ever landed, most likely by American government agents concerned about protecting their covert support of the operation. A terrified Mendel then returned to Sitka to hide out with disastrous result.

We are far from the loopy adventures of Ethan and his Yellow Brick Road Gang. Landsman learns from television reports that the Dome of the Rock has in fact been bombed. He stares at the grim image: "Broad, empty mesa of paving stone. The jagged jawbone of burnt teeth. The magnificent plume of black smoke" (358). His knowledge of the Peril Island training facility, and more particularly of the American government's support, suddenly makes him a player. He goes to government agents and deals: to maintain his silence, he wants a green card, the chance to remain in Sitka after the Reversion. Like Ethan, like Dorothy Gale, he wants a home, putting his and Bina's happiness (they have reunited) ahead of his integrity and his conscience. Of course in the end, in classic noir fashion, Landsman will not maintain such compromised ethics. As the novel closes he is contacting a newspaper reporter, and he and Bina prepare to face the difficult reality of a fast-approaching exile: "no home, no future, no fate but Bina" (411). We are far from the raucous heroics that close *Summerland.* Meyer Landsman has successfully solved the case, reunited with the love of his life, and maintained the integrity of his own code of ethics. But the two prepare in the closing pages to face a most uncertain here and now. They are now rootless, homeless, their future uneasily suspended among increasingly darker possibilities. My homeland, Landsman says, "is in my hat" (368).

Unlike *Summerland* then, *The Yiddish Policemen's Union* is a tale of a home lost. But Chabon offers to us what is lost to his characters: a kind of home that is far more durable, far more stable, and far more sheltering than the improvised homeland of Jewish Sitka. Namely he provides a gorgeously complicated plot. Chabon invests much in the political import of a Jewish home-state, and the intricate terrorist backstory involving the destruction of the Dome of the Rock surely addresses the urgency with which the displaced can resort to grand acts of violence (a sobering lesson not lost on Chabon's post–September 11th culture). But *The Yiddish Policemen's Union* is less a political tract, less a defense of a Jewish state, less even a murder mystery, than it is a dispassionate examination of the logic and soundness of plots, the construction of events into a convincing pattern of causality, the heroic effort to re-form raw event into inevitability. Chabon's narrative is heavy with schemers whose plots seek to shape and direct events against the terrifying uncertainty of contingency, the blind stroke of chance, and the hard intrusion of surprise. Consider the myriad of plots Chabon tests, tracks, and exposes: the rogue terrorists' intrigue to restage nothing less than Revelation;

the cumbersome bureaucratic protocols of police investigation that Landsman only grudgingly follows—indeed he is suspended midway through the investigation and as he continues the investigation anyhow he must flash not his badge but rather his sorry, chewed union membership card; harsh unwritten street law set down by the black-hatted Verbover; the bittersweet Jewish narrative of the Messiah figure that gives hope to each successive generation; the poignant premise of marriage; the grim counter-narrative of abortion; the desperate escape into drugs and alcohol; the intricate game-world of chess; even the Nazi's horrific Final Solution. The narrative teems with plots—some modest, some grandiose, some benign, some malevolent. Each tidy construct is intended to clarify event into logic, to contain and control the vulnerability of the here and now. But each, in turn, fails. Ultimately the sole plot construction that refuses to collapse under the weight of its own insufficiency, the only plot still intact at narrative close, is the gorgeous matrix of Chabon's own sweeping narrative, its architecture reassuringly resilient despite the sheer scale and the reach of its fabulous vision. After several false starts and abandoned manuscripts, Chabon ultimately elected to set the entire narrative in the durable resiliency of the present tense. Events unfold with a gorgeous, sumptuous immediacy, unthreatened, a here and now beyond the reach of time and space.

Of course we cannot stay within the sheltering consolation of this—or any—narrative. (Should we miss the point, Landsman has a deathly fear of closed-in spaces and must overcome his claustrophobia in order to crack the case.) We recall that Chabon's working title for his Alaskan fantasy was *Hotzeplotz*, a kind of Yiddish slang term for a remote nowhere like Podunk or Timbuktu, a place somewhere way out in the sticks, at the ends of the earth. Like Meyer Landsman and Bina, we must turn at last to face the ever-uncertain present, our temporary and fragile home lost. We are reminded of the chess game that Mendel, the dead Messiah, left behind, not so much as a clue to the killer's identity (which Landsman initially thinks it must be) as a poignant kind of suicide note, a final revelation about Mendel's desperate turn to self-destruction. Late in the narrative, himself a chess aficionado, Landsman thinks back on the crime scene and in a moment of stunning clarity understands the import of the chess game Mendel staged before his death. Mendel arranged the pieces in what is known as the Zugzwang Dilemma, a chess strategy that leaves the hapless player with no good moves, the only moves left ending in inevitable checkmate. "He can't move without finishing himself" (400). In the despondent faux-Messiah and the clear-eyed Landsman, we are offered two choices familiar to veteran readers of Chabon—surrender or engagement—when, as reader, we must reluctantly close up the magnificently structured book. We leave the contained and controlled text-site where, as in a theme park, every turn, every surprise, every twist has been carefully choreographed, and we are forced to move when no good move actually exists. We are left exactly where Landsman ends: a conclusion just shy of a happy ending. But it is far from bleak. We end on Dorothy's third heel-click, suspended, uneasy, left to accept exile as Meyer Landsman must. We depart the fabulous narrative this time as reluctant exiles who had for a time been part of a most inviting, most convincing here and now. For more than 400 pages we have been like Lear's courageous little Jumblies. And so we disembark the sturdy-fragile sieve-boat, eyes wider, hearts larger, and lives fuller for the adventure.

CHAPTER 7

Gentlemen of the Road and *Telegraph Avenue*

Despite its slender heft, *Gentlemen of the Road* (2007) has a goofy spaciousness. Chabon's cleverly crafted road novel is a buddy tale that appears on its face less an adventure story and more an extravagant celebration of the unfettered imagination. It serves as a leisurely indulgence of yarn-spinning, a generous flexing of the storytelling muscle, a novel that fashions a sturdy if entirely symbolic inkscape into which readers can happily retreat. Originally published in fifteen successive weekly installments in the Sunday *New York Times Magazine* from January to May 2007, the narrative indeed has an inviting, leisurely feel to it. Unlike *The Yiddish Policemen's Union* or even the extravagant fantasy of *Summerland, Gentlemen of the Road* lacks the steadying presence of any realistic characters. No engagingly nerdy adolescent struggles with the trauma of a mother's death. No curmudgeonly middle-aged detective tries to rekindle a lost marriage. Instead Chabon deftly animates two cut-outs who are not so much nuanced characters as loving homages to stock characters drawn from the swashbuckling adventure novels of Alexandre Dumas, Rudyard Kipling, Edgar Rice Burroughs, and Rider Haggard and from the fabulous pages of a more contemporary grand master of fantasy adventures, Michael Moorcock. Chabon readily, even gratefully, acknowledged these influences and dedicated *Gentlemen of the Road* to Moorcock.

He sets his yarn in medieval Russia, in the foothills of the Caucasus Mountains on the southwestern shores of the Caspian Sea along the dangerous routes of the fabulous Silk Road. The kaganate of Khazaria is a nearly forgotten Jewish empire-state that flourished briefly amid the larger persecutions of Jews throughout Europe, a kind of real-life version of Meyer

Landsman's Protectorate of Sitka. The narrative recounts the adventures of Zelikman and Amran, a decidedly odd couple, the most recent manifestation of similar dyads across Chabon's fictions—Arthur Lecomte and Art Bechstein; Grady Tripp and James Leer; Sammy Clay and Joe Kavalier; Ethan Feld and Jennifer T. Rideout; Meyer Landsman and Berko Shemets. As Chabon pointed out to me in a November 2012 email exchange, "personality, consciousness itself" cannot be constructed except in the plural, identifying the underlying template, the "ur-dyad" if you will, for his career-long interrogation of character as a plural construction, like the dynamic between Sherlock Holmes and Dr. Watson that so enthralled him as a child. Here the dyad is striking: Zelikman and Amran are two cunning and charismatic Jewish rogues who fancy themselves "gentlemen of the road." Zelikman is a moody, introspective Bavarian physician, pale-skinned and rail-thin with long, stringy blonde hair, distant. A twenty-something virgin, he allows himself to love only his fancy hats and his faithful horse. He is an atheist given to cynicism as a survival strategy, a loner prone to staring into campfires and smoking hemp seed and honey in an Irish dudeen, a man haunted by the murders of his mother and sister in Frankfurt during one of the frequent government-sponsored anti-Jewish pogroms. Amran is an intimidating and blood-thirsty Ethiopian mercenary—he swings a massive Viking ax dubbed "The Defiler of Your Mother." Considerably older than Zelikman and gray-haired, he is given to stoic speculations on humanity's moral corruption, which he blames on rampaging and very real demons. He is haunted by the brutal kidnapping and subsequent disappearance of his only daughter years earlier.

The narrative is rollicking (not an adjective often applied to Chabon's fiction) and follows the wild and often violent adventures of these two mismatched scoundrels. Although they feud like an old married couple, their alliance is a secure and profound friendship. The two are inadvertently swept up into a dangerous intrigue designed to restore a highly unlikeable prince named Filaq to the throne of the Kingdom of Arran after the sitting king, the prince's father, and most of his family are summarily executed by the treacherous Buljan, a marauding warlord bent only on seizing power. In the opening pages, an emissary from the deposed court attempts to hire Zelikman and Amran as security muscle to return the prince to what is left of his family. Unfortunately the emissary is ambushed and killed (an arrow through his throat) by Buljan's shadowy soldiers who are trailing the prince. Our two gentlemen of the road, uncomplicated by political alliances much less scruples, decide to escort the prince safely back to his hometown and to his wealthy family as a way of securing what they presume will be a hefty reward. Filaq, however, is interested only in avenging his family's murder. He wants to kill Buljan himself and then, with the help of a tiny but courageous remnant loyalist army, restore his family's position by securing the throne for his much beloved older brother, Alp, who was kidnapped during the coup. Such ambitious revenge is clearly at odds with Zelikman and Amran's far more practical plan. They physically restrain the young prince with a lengthy leather cord to discourage his clumsy attempts at flight.

And so the adventure begins. The narrative plot is unabashedly action-centered—the trio find the prince's town burned to the ground by Buljan's troops. Filaq is subsequently captured by Buljan's men as is Amran when he attempts to save the deposed prince. Disguised as a wealthy slave trader, Zelikman engages Buljan in court in a charade to purchase the massive Ethiopian and then dramatically frees Amran as he is about to be pulled apart by horses. The two rogues take refuge in an elegant brothel along the waterfront and plot their strategy. In the story's most compelling plot twist, however, Buljan's troops deliver to the brothel's front steps a woman, who was beaten and raped by the warlord's men. In a patented coincidence peculiar to this genre of fiction, it turns out the woman is none other than Filaq, who was apparently masquerading as a man. Zelikman and Amran tenderly minister to the brutalized girl. Amran sees his long-lost daughter in the girl's sorrowful eyes, and Zelikman begins to feel the first awkward stirrings of an infatuation for the headstrong girl. Determined now to help Filaq restore her brother to the throne, the two journey to secure the help of the kagan, the mysterious Oz-like spiritual leader of the kingdom. The kagan's unexpectedly generous support of their endeavor helps Zelikman and Amran cement an alliance with Khazan's remaining army of archers and broadswords men and, more important, its mighty armada of forty-nine intimidating war elephants.

It is at that point that Filaq is told that her brother has died of some virulent plague while in captivity. Devastated, she is determined despite her gender to claim the throne herself, against tradition. In an unabashedly grand climax, Buljan is ambushed by the reinvigorated Khazan army and, at the moment he prepares to dispatch Filaq with a broadsword, is killed ingloriously. An enraged war elephant hoists him high in the air and slams him to the ground repeatedly, "ensuring the fracture of skull and vertebrae," his body a "mass of pulp and leather."[1] In the heady wake of the victory, Filaq and Zelikman, both virgins, consummate their love awkwardly but intensely. As Chabon draws the story to its close, Filaq prepares to assume the throne and the two gentlemen of the road, amply rewarded, prepare to return to their peripatetic life, "unmindful whether [the road] turned east or south, their direction a question of no interest to either of them" (196). Wrapped in thick fur robes against the elements, the two take the first road they find that leads out of the city and head off into the beckoning sunrise. Cue the slow dissolve.

With its exotic setting, its vivid cast of engaging cartoon-characters, deft manipulations of the clichés of the swashbuckler, tangled plot of clandestine alliances and palace realpolitik, graphic violence, and heroic chronicle of a campaign to right an evident wrong, Chabon's narrative is deliberately cinematic in its execution. Chabon even engaged the talents of no less than Gary Gianni, who had for years provided the elegant line drawings of the Prince Valiant syndicated comic strip, to enhance the storyline with fifteen handsome drawings, one in each chapter, that storyboard the action and provide a visual enchantment. Thus the reader inevitably engages Chabon's plot through the means of cinema. Readers may feel a nearly irresistible urge to "cast" the two main characters. Amran alternates between the dry, sardonic menace of a Samuel L. Jackson and the quiet confidence and sheer physical command of a Denzel Washington. Zelikman alternates between the world-weary fortitude of a young Harrison Ford and the brooding heroics of a Nicolas Cage. The narrative stays wonderfully free of the buzz-kill responsibility of extracting weighty themes, which is unlike *The Yiddish Policemen's Union* with its investigation into the dynamics of a troubled marriage and its exploration of the implications of anti-Semitism or *Summerland* with its anatomy of a child handling the too-early death of a mother.

Here Chabon sings, happily free of such gravitas—save the reassurance that bad people do bad things and that good people triumph in the end. It is supremely about story, one that is giddy with its own clichés, and contains a studied prose style that is at once high-caloric, ornate, and deliberately purplish. Chabon's stylistic ventriloquism, replete with archaic vocabulary and elaborate architectural syntax, reflects his immersion in the classic adventure tales of a century earlier. You cannot *not* be aware you are reading. Given the original weekly publication strategy, each chapter ends on a wonderfully hokey and yet irresistibly charged cliffhanger. More to the point, the plot freely manipulates wild coincidences as the two wily rogues are separated and then reunited, always under tense circumstances, creating forward movement and insistent momentum. And that apparently is Chabon's point. He wants his blasé, so-sophisticated post-post-everything reader to be caught up in a story, like some wide-eyed child first strolling about the enchantments of an inviting theme park. The narrative offers an exotic retreat from the vulnerabilities and vicissitudes of the day-to-day. Happily *Gentlemen of the Road* hoodwinks the all-too-eager consumer of the artifact into surrendering to the magic of an imaginative construct that appears so sturdy.

Of course such a narrative—wonderfully executed, if decidedly lightweight escapist fare—can simply be savored as a gesture of an accomplished novelist's generosity, readers happily conceding to the charms of Chabon's yarn. Yet something troubles. Chabon is not content here to merely indulge his storytelling competencies, to simply spin an attractive story. Despite *Gentlemen of the Road*'s feel as an exuberant entertainment, Chabon sets such frothy foolishness against the narrative's far weightier imperative. Even as he indulges his love of high-octane storytelling, he acknowledges its poignant risks, its heartbreaking disappointment. *Gentlemen of the Road* is less a synthesis of Chabon's decade-long exploration of the imagination's reach and more a kind of prequel to his landmark work *Telegraph Avenue* (2012), which is a bold narrative of reentry rather than escape.

Then despite its apparent fluffiness, *Gentlemen of the Road* is a contested narrative in which its own characters are strikingly at odds with their narrative's evident ambition: the indulgence of escape into the imagination. In the fabulous narrative world of Zelikman and Amran, responsibilities and confrontation beckon the characters. Even as the reader relishes the quiet thrill of escape, the characters return to duty one by one, turning to the world and embracing its unsuspected richness. After all, unlike the four alternate worlds that Ethan Feld explores or even the mean streets of the Protectorate of Sitka, Khazaria, for all its apparent exoticism, was historically real. Chabon never misses a chance to direct his narrative and his characters toward commitment to that real world. In an unguarded moment when Filaq first receives the heartbreaking news that her brother has died alone and sick in captivity, she recalls the last time she had seen him: in the splendid gloaming of a late summer's evening when, happy and contented amid the cicadas and grapevines, they had spent the day falcon-ing. Despite her brave regal front, feeling distraught and suddenly vulnerable, Filaq is on the verge of tears. However, she happens to spy on an ornate bookstand *The Book of Roads and Kingdoms,* the handsomely illustrated classic work of the ninth-century Persian geographer Ibn Khordadbeh in which he catalogued the "miracles and wonders" not of some fabulous invented kingdoms but rather the wonders of the states in the Orient, most notably Japan and Korea. The wonders are gathered from the Persian's meticulous notes from his own travels, "page after page of cities to visit and peoples to live among . . . out there, beyond the margins of her life, along the roads and in the kingdoms," a helpful reminder of the promise of the real world itself (167). Suddenly steeled in her resolution, Filaq prepares to engage rather than flee the world, to avenge her brother and reclaim the throne.

Thus in a storyline about restoring a rightful throne, that pattern of returning to the real world fashions a kind of insurgent counter-narrative. Of all things reality emerges as the unlikely hero of this fabulous yarn. Zelikman, for instance, is a doctor. Despite all his wily confidence-man charades and the duo's elaborate stings, he is never far from the very real responsibilities of his calling, ministering to the bloodied casualties of Buljan's brutal campaign. Characters hunger for that dangerous and unpredictable real world, full of violence and rape, slavery and greed. The Oz-like kagan agrees to lend his support to the campaign to dethrone Buljan only on the condition that Zelikman and Amran concoct an elaborate ruse to convince those who guard him, those who serve in his remote palace, that he has in fact died. This liberates him at long last from a fantastic realm that had long ago become a life of confinement—he wants only to be free to return to the real world. In the end Filaq and Zelikman and Amran each opt to engage rather than withdraw. Filaq prepares to assume the heavy duties of the throne, and Zelikman and Amran decline to remain within her protection and instead return to the unpredictable adventures of the open road.

In his afterword to *Gentlemen of the Road,* Chabon offers a marvelously self-deprecating apologia for penning such an exotic adventure tale when he himself had lived a modest life in which adventure had been confined to the cliché suburban thrills of white-water rafting or the occasional extravagant weekend in Las Vegas. Tongue decidedly in cheek, he admits he has never swung a battle-ax or a broadsword, never laughed in the face of death, never escaped from prison. But Chabon closes with a cautionary observation that could serve as a revealing segue into the compassionate and humane argument of *Telegraph Avenue,* a novel that was even then in the earliest stages of its evolution. Chabon recalls a pivotal moment in Old Testament history (Genesis 12:1) when God spoke what Chabon calls the "true First Commandment" to an aging Abram (later Abraham). The man was most reluctant to leave the security and familiarity of his homeland to lead the Jewish people in an improbable flight to some promised land of milk and honey. God said to the hesitant Abram, "*lech lecha,*" which translates as the hard and clean directive "Go." The command is stern and in turn became part of the Jewish cultural identity and its heritage of perpetual Diaspora, a reminder that the fetching promise of home and the enticing premise of roots was at best problematic. That unyielding directive indicates to Chabon where his fictional sensibility has been moving since Art Bechstein's clumsy retreat. Adventure, he has come to argue, is not found in the elaborate dodge of the imagination, not in the calculated retreat into books, a "bundle of wood pulp, sewn and glued and stained with blobs of pigment and resin," but rather in the gutsy decision to engage (204). Chabon freely translates God's imperative: "Thou shalt leave home. Thou shalt get lost. Thou shalt find slander, oppression, opportunity, escape, and destruction. Thou shalt, by definition, find adventure" (203). After three decades of sanctioning characters staking out private territories, defining shelters, seeking model worlds and the safe havens of the imagination, drawing tight and clean boundaries, intimidated by reality, relaxing into strategies of retreat, finding comfort (even happiness) living apart in hidey holes and basements, garages and bedrooms, libraries and classrooms, backyards and movie theaters, it was time, Chabon intoned, to leave such splendid "homes."

Thus there is less a valedictory look-backward feel to *Telegraph Avenue* (2012) and more a liberating look ahead. It bears a text-for-the-new-millennium feel that signals Chabon, still in his early fifties, may just now be defining his mature vision. Like Whitman's *Leaves of Grass,* Steinbeck's *The Grapes of Wrath,* Ginsburg's *Howl,* Pynchon's *Vineland* and *Against the Day* (texts Chabon glosses here), *Telegraph Avenue* is decidedly big-hearted, addressed to no less than American culture itself. It is less the intimate narratives of Chabon's signature work and more a kind of manifesto vision offered to a troubling and troubled culture that Chabon clearly perceives to be in a crisis of fragmentation. He is interested in how the imagination can cross rather than defend boundaries, transcend rather than define and protect divides, how it can at once create and celebrate community, define commonality, and embrace fluidity. To echo a line that becomes something of a reprise in *Telegraph Avenue,* it is time to get real. After the decade-long excursion into the fabulous realms conjured by his unfettered imagination, Chabon returns now to his own era (*Telegraph Avenue* is set in 2004) and to his very own neighborhoods of northern California around San Francisco. Telegraph Avenue is a major thoroughfare in the Bay Area, a kind of "ragged fault line where the urban plates of Berkeley and Oakland subducted."[2] The broad boulevard roughly demarcates a socioeconomic border between the predominantly white upper-class university world of Berkeley and the blue-collar, working-class, largely African American neighborhoods of North Oakland. But Chabon tackles the business of defying rather than abiding borders. His imagination brashly defies the most deeply entrenched and hotly defended borders that have fragmented an anxious post–September 11th American culture: race, religion, education, ethnicity, political affiliation, sexual orientation, and income.

As formidable as they may appear, such barriers are merely bugaboos of the unimaginative. After a decade of using the broad reach of the imagination to defy the borders of genre—playfully busting conventional expectations by mixing and matching sports fiction, the bildungsroman, fantasy, the murder mystery, the sci-fi alternate history, the political thriller, and the adventure epic—Chabon reconceives the power of the imagination by suggesting that it can do more than reanimate hoary literary genres. He addresses a culture weary of division, weary of the anxiety implicit in maintaining such borders, weary of the vulnerability perceived as inevitable should cultural, social, and political barriers tumble. He counsels that it is time to imagine something better, something grander, to step out, to move across, to leap beyond the cultural divisions that appear inevitable, logical, even permanent to the unimaginative. It is tempting in finishing *Telegraph Avenue* to hope well beyond the Capraesque reach of Chabon's earlier works, narratives in which his determined optimism was extended to reclaim troubled and lost characters. Here Chabon reclaims the business of the imagination, storytelling itself, to inspire, to address a culture in a dark time. At fifty Chabon is still quixotic enough—and reckless enough—to imagine a real world that can transcend the borders of bigotry, racism, class, religious intolerance, political anxieties, and war. More to the point, he interrogates the logic of such entrenched thinking.

As a result *Telegraph Avenue* is less another post-9/11 narrative and more the first post-Obama narrative. Chabon dares to shape a broad, sweeping humanism that, without apology and without irony, could stand as a towering capstone vision. To echo Obama's own campaign biography, *Telegraph Avenue* tenders the audacity of hope. Barack Obama, then an Illinois state senator on the heels of an electrifying speech at the Democratic National Convention, makes a cameo appearance in *Telegraph Avenue* at a $1,000-a-plate fundraising rally for John Kerry's presidential run. He appears just long enough to offer a troubled character, who is struggling with a divisive marriage and an unrewarding career, some off-the-cuff advice that becomes something of the novel's wisdom-mantra: Do what your heart loves. To his cultural moment, Chabon argues (much as candidate Obama did in 2008) that it is time to choose. This work of serious fiction freely blurs, among many other boundaries, the line between high and low culture. To name only a handful, Chabon references *Sanford and Son, Sesame Street,* Quentin Tarantino, Tim Burton, *Blue's Clues,* Cameron Crowe, *Jesus Christ Superstar,* the iconic Japanese monster Gamera, *Star Wars,* Bruce Lee, Warner Brothers' Tasmanian Devil, the Wu-Tang Clan, *Superfly,* and of course, because this is still Michael Chabon, *The Wizard of Oz,* Marvel comics, and *Star Trek*. Chabon keys the choice he offers to two pop tunes from the 1970s, which both figure prominently in the narrative: "It's Too Late," the doleful Carole King-Gerry Goffin classic of regret and surrender (played at an impromptu funeral service improbably held in a used record store), and "Higher Ground," Stevie Wonder's soaring gospel-tinged funk anthem (played at the Kerry fundraiser before Obama's entrance). It is on its face a simple choice: despair or hope. In all but words, Chabon asks, "Well, which is it going to be?" But if the choice is clear, Chabon knows, the choosing is anything but easy. The narrative lines of *Telegraph Avenue* are rent by fissures—deep, stubborn, and ugly—between longtime friends, between neighbors, between business partners, within families, and between spouses. And then there are the far more complicated divisions within characters, the gulf between the sins of the past and the cold fear of their discovery in the present, the tricky pull of regret, and the often wide chasm between who characters really are and who they must pretend to be around hard-hearted and judgmental others.

In what is perhaps Chabon's most accomplished and intriguing structural design to date, *Telegraph Avenue* is a fugal narrative that introduces four counter-plots in a kind of staggered simultaneity, each counter-plot hinging on a duo of its own, each plotline centered on characters who encounter divisions, distances, and must struggle with apartness. The dominant plotline centers on two longtime friends, one black, one white, who run Brokeland Records, a used record shop in the environs of Berkeley. They are two solitary men, each wary of intimacy, but united in their pursuit of preserving the lost glories of an all-but-vanished world, the trove of music their store warehouses. It is, however, a narrative of two men, friends and business partners, growing increasingly apart and fast approaching a moment of irreconcilable division. We meet first the owner, the moon-faced, mountainous Archy Stallings, a veteran of the Gulf War, an accomplished jazz bassist. Now in his late thirties, he is awkwardly coming to terms with the fast-approaching birth of his first child, an intimidating commitment that he sees only as "open-ended, eternal, and invisible" (22). In the callous logic typical of Chabon's less heroic characters since Grady Tripp, Archy is handling the increasing pressures through serial philandering and by whiling away afternoons dreaming of draining the shop's meager bank account. He imagines packing up his belongings and driving off to the beaches of Belize, there to "find a hammock and breeze, [and] eat tacos made with the meat of some large jungle rodent" (399). Archy justifies such strategic retreat by invoking the stoic wisdom of no less than Marcus Aurelius, whose little book of meditations he has read 93 times and which he constantly totes around in his back pocket. His cursory understanding of stoicism has taught him only to see to his moat, to maintain a cautious distance, to stay apart, to "be careful, find a cool dry place to stash your mind, and hang on until it [is] over" (9).

Paired with Archy Stallings is the proprietor, Nat Jaffe, older by ten years, born Jewish but now an unrepentant atheist, a jazz keyboardist, yes, but more a devoted audiophile. He is a cantankerous music snob perpetually toking on a joint and perpetually out of sorts, a collector of rare albums, a curmudgeon (compared at one point to Dickens's cranky misanthrope Scrooge). He lives more at ease within the architecture of jazz harmonies than with the most casual conversations with his customers or even with his own wife and teenage son. Long sunk into an existential funk (his motto is "Born alone. Die alone."), Nat is perpetually angry as he must engage day after grueling day a legion of insufferable fools in a world that is as inhospitable as it is absurd. Despite their apparent differences, Archy and Nat are essentially alike, two Peter Pans, two boy-men in full retreat. They are determined, in the age of CDs and Internet file sharing, to man this last-stop-before-oblivion retail outpost, a used record store, a tidy little model world where they can stubbornly cling to a past that neither one actually remembers. They are too young to remember the artists whose music they treasure but are content to be surrounded by piles of moldering vinyl, a reassuring bunker of protective nostalgia, a sinecure from the world. For twelve perilous years, Brokeland Records has held its own despite an increasingly shrinking market, specializing in archiving thousands of obscure jazz and blues titles for a rapidly narrowing neighborhood clientele. Their colorful regulars are still charmed by the uncomplicated heft and ragged acoustic quality of an album and happily linger within the store's throwback ambience, engaging in meandering bull sessions on everything from the merits of obscure jazz recording to the best raised doughnuts in the neighborhood.

But a new threat emerges: the planned construction, just two blocks away, of a massive megastore complex of boutiques, restaurants, and movie theaters. The development will include a sprawling music store specializing in brokering classic vinyl, thus ensuring the imminent demise once and for all of tiny Brokeland. The megastore complex, widely hailed as a community-revival project, is being spearheaded by one Gibson Goode, a wealthy if flamboyant Oakland native son. (He flies above the city's sprawling neighborhoods in a specially outfitted Xanadu-like airship christened the *Minnie Riperton*).[3] Goode has parlayed a successful football career as a Pro Bowl quarterback for the Pittsburgh Steelers into lucrative media business venture. (He is listed as the fifth wealthiest black man in America.) The grand megastore project has received the unexpected backing of one of the neighborhood's most notorious power brokers, part-time councilman and full-time mortician Chandler Flowers. But Chan Flowers is vulnerable. He harbors a potentially explosive secret from his distant past: an execution-style shooting more than forty years earlier of a neighborhood lowlife, a pimp and drug dealer named Popcorn Hughes, a rival to Huey Newton, then a leader of the city's Black Panther Party. Flowers viewed the shooting as a way to both distance himself from a rigid and conservative upbringing and at the same time to ingratiate himself with the party's hierarchy. Although the shooting had long ago gone cold for the police, it still haunts Flowers.

Archy's long-delayed and problematic coming of age (he is, as his name suggests, stalling) commands the center of this narrative thread. Archy begins to understand the depth of the megastore's threat against his business and sorts through the implications of his fast-approaching fatherhood, He is forced to deal with the anger of his wife, who discovers his most recent infidelity. (Distrusting his lame denials, his wife reaches into his pants and smells the sticky residue of his unfaithfulness.) He contemplates a generous offer from Gibson Goode to work at the new megastore, an invitation tendered while Archy is being given a grand ride in the skies above Oakland in Goode's floating leviathan. Even as he must consider the dire complications that accepting the offer would mean to the chronically out-of-sorts Nat, Archy comes to terms with the implications of continuing to run from reality after the traumatic experiences in the Gulf War. "I have been fucking off, fucking up, and fucking around for too long. I need to get real, else I'm going to end up living in an auto body shop. I need insurance, a paycheck, all that straight-life bullshit" (348). That awareness is brought into particularly sharp focus when his spiritual mentor and surrogate father, an eccentric sixty-something funk keyboardist named Cochise Jones, is killed suddenly in a bizarre accident. While attempting to move a Hammond B-3 organ ("diesel-heavy, coffin-awkward, clock-fragile" [130]) for the gig at the Kerry fundraiser, Cochise loses his grip and the massive instrument crushes him.

Ironically, while Archy wrestles for the first time with the implications of the absoluteness of death and the need to get real before it is too late, Cochise's death actually inspires Nat, who had been all but resigned, in his typical existential funk, to losing the store. Using Cochise's uncompromising spirit as a battle cry, Nat rallies a ragtag collection of neighborhood regulars. In the tradition of the long-ago counterculture, they mount a concerted (and manifestly doomed) campaign to preserve the little record store, claiming the megastore would destroy the neighborhood's quaint ambience and, like the cancerous spread of Walmarts, imperil the future of small businesses. But Archy does not share Nat's enthusiasm to salvage a business he now sees all too clearly as doomed. He prepares to sever their association. Increasingly frustrated and inspired by listening to the elegant "low-frequency rage" of John Coltrane's *A Love Supreme,* a very drunk Nat heads to the local airfield determined to urinate on Goode's flashy dirigible in an inspired act of vandalism (414). But carried away by the hot logic of his quixotic rebellion, he arrives at the airfield and decides to untether the airship entirely, "like in *The Wizard of Oz*" (418). He watches it drift up into the bronze sky "with appalling grace and lightness" (418). Days later it will come down harmlessly in distant Utah after Nat has been arrested for "liberating" the zeppelin. An exhilarated Nat simply walked home from the airfield, leaving his car behind—an easy trace for the police.

A second narrative line—and a second dyad—centers similarly on two friends, business associates fast approaching a fissure of their own. Berkeley Birth Partners, a thriving upscale midwife business (more than a thousand babies caught), is run by the two wives of the record store's owners: the fiery Gwen Shanks, Archy's wife, emotionally vulnerable in her final trimester of her first pregnancy, and Aviva Roth-Jaffe, Nat's wife, far more sanguine, far more pragmatic. When a routine home birth goes terribly wrong—unexpectedly heavy bleeding occurs before the afterbirth passes—the two midwives must transport the distressed woman to a nearby hospital where the placenta must be removed manually. Amid the barely concealed hostility of the hospital establishment that sees in such birthing practice a throw-back to primitive medical care, Gwen has a particularly ugly encounter with Dr. Paul Lazar. An arrogant, fish-faced obstetrician, he not only disparages the women's midwife practice but also makes snide, borderline racist remarks that infuriate Gwen. Among other insensitive asides, he compares midwifery to voodoo. The confrontation ignites a firestorm of threatened litigation not only from the parents of the newborn, who has survived the traumatic delivery, but from the hospital as well. The proud Gwen cannot bring herself to offer even an insincere apology, maintaining that she and Aviva acted appropriately and professionally. Gwen and Aviva must fight the hospital's efforts to revoke their access privileges, which would in turn doom their business. Much like her husband, Gwen begins to see the limits rather than the possibilities of her career choice, acknowledging how disillusioned she had become helping rich white women in their palatial canyon homes. She believes her spoiled clients seek a kind of faux-hipness in home delivery—all natural and without medical assistance—to one-up their friends. Gwen grows increasingly certain she would much rather use her nurse's degree to secure the privileges (and respect) of a more conventional hospital position. Even as she enters the last difficult weeks of her own pregnancy, Gwen contemplates how best to break the news to Aviva.

In the novel's two remaining narrative lines, Chabon tests the tense divisions that open up not between friends but rather within families. One line centers on the difficult reunion between Archy and his deadbeat father, the feckless Luther, whom he has not seen in more than three decades. After a long career as an international martial-arts champion, Luther became an iconic figure in the brief blaxploitation craze of the mid-1970s, playing a John Shaft–like character named Cleon Strutter. In two highly successful B-movies, Luther's agility, precision, and raw power attained for him cult status as a kind of black Bruce Lee. But fame proved short-lived. In the nearly thirty years since, Luther struggled to adjust to life without the privileges of celebrity, spiraling into chemical and alcoholic dependencies (and stints in county lock-ups) as well with the gnawing certainty that he could have been bigger, much bigger. In fact, in the narrative present, Luther returns to Oakland accompanied by his co-star, the still voluptuous Valletta Moore. He is certain that, even more than thirty years after his last starring role, the post-postmodern American film culture is primed for a third Strutter film—if only he could secure financial backing. He surfaces in Oakland as much to reunite with his estranged son as to blackmail Chan Flowers. Long ago Luther drove the getaway car the night of the shooting of Popcorn Hughes and claims that he has kept one of the gloves Flowers had worn. He is certain now that with DNA analysis he could ruin Flowers unless the wealthy undertaker pays him handsomely—$100,000, more than enough to finance *Strutter 3*.

The fourth narrative line is perhaps Chabon's most poignant. It centers on the bittersweet reunion between Archy and a teenage son he did not even know existed. The boy's mother died in a car accident years earlier back in Texas, and he had been raised by his grandmother. The sullen Titus Joyner, in a strategy that recalls other Chabon adolescents compelled to survive a traumatic childhood, has long relied on the aesthetic shelter-escape of the movies. Only fourteen, he is an aspiring and precocious auteur who has already completed five film scripts. One is based on the Ambrose Bierce war story "Incident at Owl Creek Bridge," a bittersweet interrogation into the power of the imagination to temporarily stave off a difficult reality. He comes to California as much to meet his father and to perhaps find a new family as to immerse himself in the region's rich culture of movies. (He is bowled over when he discovers that his grandfather is in fact the iconic Cleon Strutter.) During a night class on the films of Quentin Tarantino, Titus becomes fast friends with Nat Jaffe's son, Julius (called Julie), a forlorn and melancholic misfit who is struggling to find himself. Among other quirks, he distributes specially printed mock-business cards, each with a different name. For his part, Julie is dealing with his emerging suspicions that he is if not gay then certainly bi-curious.

Only gradually becoming aware of the ties between their fathers, the two misfits strike up a most unconventional relationship and Titus moves in with the Jaffes. The relationship quickly turns heated and quite sexual (although a surly Titus denies he is gay and delights in spouting disparaging anti-gay rhetoric even after the two have had sex). After Archy and Titus endure a delicate introduction, Titus seeks only acceptance. And once he knows who his grandfather is, Titus is mesmerized by DVDs of the vintage Strutter movies. He encourages Archy to watch them, to appreciate the artistry and the physical eloquence of his father. But it is not easy for Archy to accept a full-grown son. He struggles to come to terms with "all that resentfulness and abandonment" (154). And there is the problem of telling the emotionally wired Gwen. In a moment of fortuitous coincidence, an agitated and distracted Gwen (she is on her way to a meeting with lawyers following the botched delivery) tries to flag down a city bus along busy Telegraph Avenue by stepping out into the street. Titus, who happens to be riding by on his bike, has just enough time to push the very pregnant Gwen out of the way of an oncoming bus, saving her life. In quick order, Gwen is introduced to Titus and understands that he is her husband's son. Stunned and rapidly approaching her due date, she promptly moves out to rethink her marriage to a man she sees now is an irredeemable dog. Gwen seeks the security and protection of a safe house, in this case a neighborhood martial-arts dojang run by a wizened Chinese kung fu master named Irene Jew. (Irene counts among her past students both Bruce Lee and Luther Stallings.) There in safe sanctuary, and typical of so many Chabon signature characters, Gwen contemplates the urge to flee, to "light out for someplace," anyplace (288).

Each of the four plotlines moves toward the trauma of division. Businesses collapse, friendships dissolve, families divide. But the long and difficult birth of Gwen and Archy's baby that closes the book compels the narrative's magisterial ascent toward union and reunion. When Gwen's water breaks, she is with young Julie and Nat, who is just back from liberating the zeppelin. Of course Nat is a most unpromising birthing partner. But when Gwen emerges from a restroom, her clothes spattered, he sees in her face a vulnerability to which he immediately, instinctively responds. "He understood that she was about to set out for a place, come what may, where she would be completely alone, so much more alone than an existential drama queen like

Nat could possibly imagine" (422). He is determined to violate that apartness. Despite knowing next to nothing about the birthing process, he is determined to be her substitute coach in the absence of her husband Archy, who is even then brokering the showdown deal between Luther and Chan Flowers, and without Aviva who, in a snit over Gwen's determination to break up the business, is attending a birth elsewhere. So it is up to Nat. The three head to the hospital.

There Chabon records without flinching, without recourse to clichés or euphemisms, the raw birth experience. We share the tearing heat of Gwen's contractions; the hard rhythms of her heroic pushing (each rest a "patch of blue sky between two rolling thunderheads" [446]); her involuntary expelling of bodily fluids (the bed is drenched, swampy); her heart-wrenching anxieties over the well-being of the fast-approaching baby (despite her vast experience with catching babies, this is after all Gwen's first delivery). Her archenemy, the fish-faced Dr. Lazar, is on duty and responds to the birthing alert, standing by in case of complications. Urgent calls are made to summon both Archy and Aviva, but the novice Nat will be her coach. "He leaned in, reaching toward her, hunching the way he hunched over the keys of a piano" (451). And then in a most dramatic moment, she delivers a son. We feel the invigorating relief and the enormous emotional impact. The implications of being a new mother are as immediate as they are compelling: "All the anger that Gwen had been feeling, not just over today or over the past nine months but all her life—feeding on it like a sun, using it to power her engines, to fund her stake in the American dream—struck her for the first time as a liability. As purely tragic. There was no way to partake of it without handing it down the generations" (451). That sweeping epiphany, as natural and as unforced (and as painful and as hard-earned) as the delivery itself, will shape and direct the narrative's conclusion.

We move forward five weeks. Much has changed. Determined now to create a family, Gwen has reconciled with Archy, although they both acknowledge that forgiveness will take time. "One day, he hoped, this foreordained path would lead, amid countless chutes and precious few ladders to the square of ultimate redemption—Forgiveness" (453). For now, the four of them—Gwen, the newborn, Archy, and Titus—have begun the work of shaping a family across what had seemed impossible divisions. Gwen has moved forward professionally. Without the intrusive presence of lawyers, Gwen simply drives to the home of the family whose baby had gone into fetal distress. There, while the father is painting the baby's new crib, the two simply talk. Now on the other side of her own delivery experience, Gwen sincerely apologizes—not for any professional incompetence but rather for allowing herself to be distracted by her showdown with the imperious Dr. Lazar. It was the critical moment in the hospital when the baby—and its mother—most needed her. His wife and his child both happy and healthy, the father unconditionally accepts Gwen's heartfelt apology. He in turn offers to drop the lawsuit. Gwen also goes forward with her decision to pursue a medical degree, to take the MCAT, to abandon the home-delivery business entirely (to leave home as it were), and to engage the broader challenge of hospital work. As she tells a disappointed Aviva, "I'm sick of having no power in the game . . . and them having it all. Of always fighting against feeling useless" (404).

For his part Archy completes his own movement into the real world. He decides to leave retail entirely, abandon the cozy shelter-house of Brokeland, and pursue a real-estate license. We learn that when his father admits to Chan Flowers that he lost the incriminating glove years earlier and that the entire blackmail scheme was an elaborate bluff, a relieved Chan offers to help Archy by using his influence to redirect the megastore project to a different, more distant neighborhood. But Archy is determined not to return to the hidey-hole of Brokeland. In a moment of pragmatic charity, Archy offers to sell Brokeland Records and give what he can to help his father finance the third Strutter film. And even the misanthropic Nat turns (like Scrooge at the casement window Christmas morning) to a wider, broader perspective. As the narrative closes, Archy, now a licensed real estate agent, is showing a typically recalcitrant Nat an available property for a new store site, a more attractive and far more contemporary storefront along Telegraph Avenue. Naturally Nat is unimpressed by what he dismisses as the sterile modern feel of the new site (although it was built in the 1920s). But Archy patiently convinces the Luddite Nat about the limitless possibilities that would come from using the site only as a base of operations, ultimately putting the vinyl record business online, opening the archive to an international community of audiophiles. Nat sees clearly the implications. "I have to get real *and* take shit seriously? . . . At the same time?" (459). And even Julius and Titus, for their part, share in the narrative's redemptive movement. They have maintained their friendship, despite going off to different schools. They meet nightly within the Internet's vast gaming world. (Now liberated into his bisexuality, Julie plays a fetching girl character named Dezire online). Nat dutifully heads out to pick up garbage as part of his community-service hours after his conviction for malicious mischief for untying the zeppelin. His crazy dream to run off to Belize abandoned for the deep satisfactions of being a faithful husband and a hands-on father, Archy happily drives off with both his sons in a decidedly uncool "drag-ass, baby-smelling, style-free Subaru wagon" (464).

On a whim Archy decides to drive past the old Brokeland Store—it is now a trading card shop. Archy ruminates without souring irony about the viability of the neighborhood itself, how failed stores concede in a kind of urban version of Darwinian evolution to newer, better stores. He considers how despair gives way to hope as a neighborhood maintains and survives: the "new operation held promise, and in principle, at least he approved" (465). And we close with the affirmation as much directed to Chabon's own cultural community as to Archy's Oakland: "It was all about the neighborhood; that space where common sorrow could be drowned in common passion as the talk grew ever more scholarly and wild" (465). Characters have stopped running away and have instead engaged. Protective "homes" have been abandoned to engage the uncertain promise of wider experience. We are reminded of a moment Gwen recalls when a ten-year-old Julie, as precocious as any of Chabon's wounded adolescent misfits since Nathan Shapiro, delivered an impromptu lecture on the definition of pantropy. It is a grand theory particular to his sci-fi universe in which humans adapt both physically and mentally to harsh and unforgiving environments, a process of adjusting, of rugged and determined engagement that in the end would "allow survival, even prosperity" (287). In the choice between hope and despair, Chabon's characters, one by one, embrace hope, decide to overcome resentment, abandon the simple strategy of escape, and engage the real world. They move beyond pettiness and selfishness, defy apparently insurmountable divisions, breach the limits of melodramatic rage and self-absorbed angst, and find their way to tiny, fragile gestures of kindness, consideration, respect, and love. Their actions reanimate the everyday world of kids and bills, of work and routine, with the energy of modest possibility. It is not a happy ending, a phrase that smacks of unearned optimism and tacked-on, feel-good shallowness. Call it pantropic adjustment instead, gestures as courageous as they are necessary.

But amid characters who so heroically defy boundaries, who so boldly catapult over divisions, it is easy to overlook the most heroic defiance of all: Chabon himself. In what is nearly the novel's centerpiece, chapter 3, Chabon risks abandoning the compelling (and realistic) narrative lines entirely for what can be dismissed as a snarky act of residual postmodern gimmickry. In a twelve-page prose tour de force, a single tsunamic sentence free of narrow grammatical niceties, he records the free flight of a rare African grey parrot, the longtime companion of Cochise Jones. (The musician's signature gaudy leisure suits all bore the unmistakable imprint of claw marks on their shoulders from the bird's constant perching.) In the wake of its longtime owner's sudden death, the bird is freed by Jones's relatives, who are uncertain exactly what to do with the bird. Fifty-Eight, the bird's gnomic name, has long maintained a quasi-spiritual, Buddha-like presence, radiating a kind of keen spiritual energy. "Restless as a radio telescope, the parrot's head with its staring eye plowed the universe for invisible signs and messages" (32).

The chapter follows the bird as it soars above the neighborhoods of Telegraph Avenue. He moves with graceful ease, perch to perch, among and between all the characters Chabon has introduced, merging their individual predicaments into a single grand sentence. The chapter foreshadows a moment late in the narrative when the nerdy Julie, in a desperate effort to try to distract Gwen during the worst of her contractions, talks Trekkie to her, including mimicking a Vulcan mind meld. Within Trekkie folklore, it is an act of aggressive cerebral assertion in which Spock, the starship's hyperintellectual Vulcan science officer, would merge his consciousness with another's, dramatically transgressing the apparent absolute boundary of individual identity. Chapter 3 is just such a bracing transgression, the reader giddy with the bird's unfettered freedom, the adrenaline rush of embracing momentum that re-creates, in language, a single entity, the neighborhood as a grand Whitmanesque entity, a single organism. All the complicated tragedies and dilemmas of the characters meld under the parrot's restless eye into a single unified energy field. It is a rendering in pulsing liberated prose of oneness, a grand defiance of divisions.

Far from some narrative gimmick, however, Fifty-Eight's crazy flight is precisely what Chabon does as narrator. Dispensing with the claustrophobic intimacies and inherent limitations of first-person, here Chabon opens his narrative voice to a soaring, wildly invasive third-person omniscience that is at once exhilarating and daring. Restless, observant, open, Chabon uses the privilege of third-person to inhabit characters, unlicensed, unsponsored, defying barriers and soaring beyond boundaries. Consider what he inhabits. He is in turn a black street thug, a promising teenage film student, an adolescent bisexual, a Gulf War veteran, a very pregnant black woman, an insensitive obstetrician, a low-octane, wannabe lawyer, a Jewish midwife, a calculating ward pol, a committed atheist, a crabby jazz aficionado, a world-weary Buddhist martial-arts master, a fabulously wealthy black entrepreneur, a blaxploitation has-been—even an exotic bird. Chabon is at once none of them and all of them. It is a most formidable trespass, after more than a generation in which the fiercely promulgated doctrine of political correctness and its uncompromising demand for the respect for diversity had largely segregated the human experience into individual experiences, that is, narrow identities defined by (and restricted to) religion, economic class, political affiliation, sexual orientation, and ethnicity. Political correctness defined and then insisted on the integrity of such cultural divisions and the need to guard those distances between peoples or run the risk of being accused of cultural trespass and unlicensed imperialism. Chabon uses the license of the imagination to soar beyond, around, and into characters whose backgrounds are distinctly not his—with impudence and without apology, he inhabits the consciousness of blacks, entrepreneurs, women, youth, the rich, the poor, gays, atheists, the under-educated.[4] Like the vinyl records that Brokeland handles, here all these individual grooves together create the splendid sonic effect of vibrant music. Chabon's narrative authority is akin to the needle that generates the sonic harmony. *Telegraph Avenue,* then, is more than well-meaning ventriloquism. It recalls the landmark works of redemptive realism of more than a century ago in which writers from Balzac to Faulkner invoked the outreach of the imagination to use storytelling to cross lines, to create the difficult harmonics of a human community.

In perhaps the novel's most touching set piece, an emotionally devastated Archy, struggling with the emotional impact of losing his mentor so suddenly, offers a poignant (and lengthy) eulogy at Cochise Jones's funeral service, held among his friends at the record store. Archy describes how Cochise grew up just outside of New Orleans listening to the city's panoply of music styles. He refused to narrow his experience to a single genre or to a single sound but rather had opened himself up to "church music, jump music, rock and roll, hard bop, soul-jazz" (373). He knew nothing of the labels and isms but simply invested in the sound, the energy, the rhythm, the visceral touch of the music. In long conversations in the record store, Archy recalls, Cochise described his own musical stylings as "Brokeland Creole," which Archy tries to define even as he fights tears. Because it best defines Chabon's conception of narrative and the power of the imagination to defy rather than maintain boundaries, Archy's passionate remarks merit quoting at length:

> "That means you stop drawing those lines. It means Africa and Europe cooked up in the same skillet. Chopin, hymns, Irish music, polyrhythms, talking drums. And people. . . . There's a sort of a, what, an ideal that I know Nat and me always had in mind for the store. Not, like, anything we ever planned out or talked about. But it's something like this: on the old Silk Road, you know, between Europe and China. It's all tribes and deserts, and then you've got this long, hard journey, take you a couple of years to get there if you go quick. It's a hard road, it has bandits,

> sandstorms. You carrying the light of civilizations back and forth. . . . Like you know how every tribe's name, when you translate it, turns out to mean 'the people.' . . . And every so often, every few hundred miles, maybe, you get these oases, right, these caravansaries, where they all get together and chill, hang out, listen to good music, swap wild tales of exaggeration" (373–74).

The nod to *Gentlemen of the Road* is all too appropriate. With the sweeping affirmation of *Telegraph Avenue,* Chabon moves his narrative vision forward into a broad, new energy and a stirring new sense of possibility. A decade earlier in the wistful closing of *Kavalier & Clay,* Chabon conceded that the imagination was ultimately powerless against the hard press of history, that narrative could not fix the world. But here the imagination emerges boldly, defiantly, as the sole energy capable of doing just that.

In an essay entitled "The Heartbreak Kid," Michael Chabon recalls a night with college buddies while he was an undergraduate at Pitt. Drinking beer, smoking marijuana, the friends indulged a typical late-night, hyper-honest bull session during which a friend kindly (if drunkenly) diagnosed Chabon's problem: he was just too happy. He lacked "*tristerza,*" sadness. As Chabon recalls, "He seemed to hold my lack of sadness against me or, rather, to pity me for that lack, and it was not long before I began to regret the absence of *tristerza* in my soul or destiny. I was by nature (whatever that means) a cheerful person, fortunate, born into comfortable circumstances during a time of unprecedented plenty, free, male, able-bodied, reasonably clever, fortunate, and willing to work. . . . Now it turned out that I was suffering from a grievous lack of *tristerza*" (*Manhood for Amateurs* 112). Although Chabon's self-deprecating tone is unmistakable, the premise of his friend's argument has long haunted Chabon's literary reputation, the charge that he is too happy, that he is lightweight because of his ingratiating chin-up optimism.

But understanding Michael Chabon means necessarily understanding the dimension, the implication of that vision, a tempered affirmation asserted against a vivid sense of what the world is capable of doing—war, greed, bigotry, selfishness, carnality, materialism, violence, meanness, a slavish obeisance to science and technology. Despair, however, can never be the last word. Chabon's mature vision is quietly, unobtrusively grounded in his mid-life reengagement of Judaism. This is not so much its doctrinal tenets, or its often uncompromising sense of its own moral rightness, or even its staunch political activism, but rather its wider, deeper apprehension of the value of suffering and its celebration of the imagination and storytelling. It is in many important ways true that Chabon cannot resist a coda. Too compassionate for irony, too generous for satire, too sympathetic for parody, Chabon, however, is in the end too grounded to indulge Disney's spectacle magic, too aware to recycle Capra's soundstage sunshine. *Telegraph Avenue* testifies to that evolution. In forty years of telling stories of misfit characters, vulnerable and anxious, who, in the end, move toward a hesitant engagement with the perplexing world of strife and brutality, Chabon ultimately understands that as a culture we endure only through a faith in the larger energy of community and a reenchantment with the real world. We use the gift of the imagination not to escape into private worlds of symbolic consolation but rather to reclaim sympathy, the difficult and uncertain movement of each to the other.

NOTES

Chapter 1—Understanding Michael Chabon

1. Although single-author treatments of contemporary (that is post-Pynchon) authors are of course rare, it is nevertheless remarkable that Chabon has generated only a single volume by Helene Meyers to date. Her book is essentially a study guide containing helpful plot summaries and character lists with only broad interest in a variety of general themes. However her slim volume has a thorough bibliography that lists many of the reviews in newspapers and magazines that Chabon received early in his career, which launched him as a wunderkind.

2. The following review of Chabon's biography is guided largely by Chabon's own writings on his website, which includes a helpful (and uproarious) timeline as well as remarks in his interviews (most notably the *Rolling Stone* piece), also archived on the website. Early on Chabon embraced the concept of honest and open celebrity and, despite his own preternatural shyness, has long cooperated with reader/fans (and critics) interested in grounding a reading of his fictions using the materials of his biography.

Chapter 2—*The Mysteries of Pittsburgh*

1. Michael Chabon, *The Mysteries of Pittsburgh* (New York: William Morrow, 1988), 52. Further references to this novel are noted parenthetically.

2. Compare, for instance, Meanor's analysis in which he concludes that Chabon offers a straightforward coming-of-age narrative and that Art emerges in the end to a position of maturity and awareness.

Chapter 3—*The Lost World* Cycle

1. See "The Success of Michael Chabon's Failure," published online in *The Quivering Pen* by novelist David Abrams for a concise overview of the crash-and-burn writing of "Fountain City." See also Chabon's website for archived sample chapters. Online buzz has long speculated that Chabon will, at some point, publish the entire manuscript.

2. Michael Chabon, *A Model World and Other Stories* (New York: HarperCollins, 1991), 26. Further references to this text are noted parenthetically.

3. For a contrasting approach, see Fowler who argues (in the first published study on Chabon) that this story cycle measures Nathan's accommodation to the real world, the adult world, rather than, as argued here, his resignation and unhappiness over what he sees as untenable compromise and flattened expectations.

4. For a different perspective, see Fowler who regards Chaya's letter as a measure not of her simple honesty but rather of her jealousy, her hurt, and her anger over Nathan's treatment of her.

Chapter 4—*Wonder Boys*

1. Michael Chabon, *Wonder Boys* (New York: Villard, 1995), 333. Further references to this novel are noted parenthetically.

2. This reading of the novel as a comic romp, an episodic picaresque novel, is made perhaps most articulately by McCulloch, although Meyers also surveys critical response and judges the book refreshingly light and wickedly fun.

Chapter 5—*Werewolves in Their Youth* and *The Amazing Adventures of Kavalier & Clay*

1. Michael Chabon, *Werewolves in Their Youth: Stories* (New York: Random House, 1999), 29. Further references to this text are noted parenthetically.

2. The debate over Michael Chabon's "Jewishness" has been an element of Chabon's work since *Kavalier & Clay*. See Meyers's chapter on the book for a solid overview. For a thoughtful analysis of the evolution of Chabon's work within the Jewish tradition, as well as Chabon's use of the metaphors and rituals of his faith, see Myers.

3. For a thorough argument of Chabon's use of comic books and the super hero, see Behlman. For a discussion of Chabon's use of history and his novel as a social-political-cultural biography of America between the wars and the decade after, see Punday.

4. Michael Chabon, *The Amazing Adventures of Kavalier & Clay* (New York: Random House, 2000), 153. Further references to this novel are made parenthetically.

5. For a contrasting reading of the Golem, see Behlman who views the fantastic figure within a broad Jewish tradition that regards the Golem as a safehouse against confronting reality, how fantasy itself is an "interruption to memory" (70). For a fascinating look at the mythic status of the Golem among the Jewish people, see Berger.

Chapter 6—*Summerland* and *The Yiddish Policemen's Union*

1. Uncertainty, perhaps unease, about Chabon's strategy for the first decade of the new century, his turn to what might appear to be dismissible lightweight entertainments, runs through many of the reviews, even laudatory ones. They suggest that perhaps he might be approached as a kind of Graham Greene figure, who also shuttled between novels of serious intent and entertainments. See Meyers for a helpful summary of the critical response. See Chabon's Afterword to *Gentlemen of the Road* and his 2005 essay "Trickster in a Suit of Lights" (reprinted in *Maps and Legends*, 13–26) for his response. See also J. Madison Davis's short piece on Chabon's mix of genres that in turn creates, or rather re-creates, popular mass-market genres into more sophisticated narrative hybrids.

2. For a most engaging and thoughtful reading of *Summerland* as a traditional sports novel—in this case one that seeks to challenge traditional gender stereotypes through the vehicle of Jennifer T. Rideout and the complicated relationship between Ethan and his father—see Colbran.

3. Michael Chabon, *Summerland* (New York: Hyperion, 2002), 416. Further references to this novel are made parenthetically.

4. In fact Chabon has drawn on a wide variety of cultural sources to create many of the characters and situations in *Summerland,* including Native American folklore, Northern European myths, traditional fairy tales, as well as echoes of Rowling, Tolkien, and C. S. Lewis.

5. Michael Chabon, *The Yiddish Policemen's Union.* (New York: HarperCollins, 2007), 17. Further references to this novel are made parenthetically.

6. Although the scope of this chapter precludes investigating Chabon's evolving interest in expanding his use of Jewish traditions in his fiction, see Myers for a critique of Chabon's use of the Yiddish language and the Yiddish traditions. For a thorough investigation into the novel's use of the Jewish state and the complicated question of Jewish political identity, see Kravitz. See also Shandler for a broad look at the concept of Yiddish literature that positions Chabon's work within that context.

Chapter 7—*Gentlemen of the Road* and *Telegraph Avenue*

1. Michael Chabon, *Gentlemen of the Road: A Tale of Adventure* (St. Paul, Minn.: Yotzeret, 2008), 188. Further references to this novel are made parenthetically.

2. Michael Chabon, *Telegraph Avenue* (New York: HarperCollins, 2012), 35. Further references to this text are made parenthetically.

3. Airships, zeppelins, and hot air balloons figure prominently throughout Chabon's fiction. Archy takes a splendid ride over the city of Oakland and later a stoned Nat liberates the same zeppelin. Ethan Feld's father works to invent a kind of family airship in *Summerland*, and much of the action in that novel is helped through the vehicle, literally, of Ethan's souped-up Saab. The Escapist travels by sleek autogyro. Chabon's fascination with the *The Wizard of Oz*—in which a hot air balloon serves as the method of transportation between the real world and the fantasy world—prompts references to the film throughout his fiction. In fact he uses a variety of birds and even clouds for the same effect. For a novelist fascinated by the tension between the real and the imagined, between engagement and escape, the symbol of the airship (and birds and clouds for that matter), at once so defiantly ethereal and yet so tethered to the ground, provides a most helpful gloss.

4. See Tanner Colby for an eloquent and provocative defense of Chabon's narrative voice as it crosses ethnic boundaries to create *Telegraph Avenue,* a reading that places Chabon within a wider tradition that dates back to William Styron's problematic achievement in *The Confessions of Nat Turner.*

BIBLIOGRAPHY

Works by Michael Chabon

BOOKS

The Mysteries of Pittsburgh. New York: William Morrow, 1988.

A Model World and Other Stories. New York: HarperCollins, 1991.

Wonder Boys. New York: Villard, 1995.

Werewolves in Their Youth: Stories. New York: Random House, 1999.

The Amazing Adventures of Kavalier & Clay. New York: Random House, 2000.

Summerland. New York: Hyperion, 2002.

The Final Solution: A Story of Detection. New York: HarperCollins, 2005.

The Yiddish Policemen's Union. New York: HarperCollins, 2007.

Gentlemen of the Road: A Tale of Adventure. St. Paul, Minn.: Yotzeret, 2008.

Maps and Legends: Reading and Writing along the Borderlands. San Francisco: McSweeney's Books, 2008.

Manhood for Amateurs: The Pleasures and Regrets of a Husband, Father, and Son. New York: HarperCollins, 2009.

Telegraph Avenue. New York: HarperCollins, 2012.

WEBSITE

www.michaelchabon.com. The Amazing Website of Kavalier & Clay, www.sugarbombs.com (accessed 2 June 2013) Invaluable compendium, run by Chabon himself, of biographical factoids, uncollected writings, current projects, and a constantly updated review of Chabon's current interests in music, film, television, literature, and cooking.

Selected Works about Michael Chabon

INTERVIEWS

Binelli, Mark. "The Amazing Story of the Comic-Book Nerd Who Won the Pulitzer Prize for Fiction: A Conversation with Michael Chabon." *Rolling Stone* 27 September 2001: 58–62, 78. An early and seminal interview, provides a hip and wide-ranging look at Chabon with particular focus on his biography, his interest in pop culture, and his investigations into sexual identity.

SELECTED CRITICAL ANALYSES

Behlman, Lee. "The Escapist: Fantasy, Folklore, and the Pleasures of the Comic Book in Recent Jewish American Holocaust Fiction." *Shofar: An Interdisciplinary Journal of Jewish Studies* 22 (Spring 2004): 56–71. Provocative look at *Kavalier*

& Clay. Argues that Chabon investigates the horrors of the Holocaust indirectly. Although clearly a work of social realism, *Kavalier & Clay* tests the vehicle of fantasy and the imaginative excess of the comic book genre as strategies to overcome history or to escape it entirely.

Berger, Alan L. "Michael Chabon's *The Amazing Adventures of Kavalier & Clay:* The Return of the Golem." *Studies in American Jewish Literature* 29 (2010): 80–89. Important analysis of the novel within the genre of fiction of the Jewish Holocaust. Argues that Chabon evokes the horrors of the Nazis indirectly using the frame of comic books and by tracing ties between the super-hero figure of the Escapist and the traditional figure of the Golem.

Colbran, Louise. "Playing at Being Men: Baseball and Masculinity in Michael Chabon's *Summerland*." *Aethlon: The Journal of Sport Literature* 25 (Fall-Winter 2007): 145–66. A compelling gender-theory analysis of *Summerland*, the work challenges traditional masculine-dominated baseball novels through the provocative character of Jennifer T. Rideout and through the emotional development of the nerdy Ethan.

Colby, Tanner. "Can a White Author Write Black Characters?" *Culturebox: Slate Magazine* Posted September 19, 2012 www.slate.com/articles/arts/culturebox.html (accessed 2 June 2013). Wide-ranging discussion of Chabon's heroic willingness to transcend racial boundaries in *Telegraph Avenue,* citing the reluctance of a generation of white writers to use the imagination. Positions Chabon among a small group of daring contemporary white writers willing to test black consciousness as a way to thaw the concept of cultural ownership and in turn explore the dimension of racism in the post–Obama era.

Davis, J. Madison. "Mix and Match: Michael Chabon's Imaginative Use of Genre." *World Literature Today* 82 (November/December 2008): 9–11. Analysis of how Chabon splices genres—the murder mystery and the alternative-history fantasy—as a way to create aesthetic distance, separating us from the postmodern fascination with exposing the bare structures of narrative and allowing us rather to embrace the plot.

Fowler, Douglas. "The Short Fiction of Michael Chabon: Nostalgia in the Very Young." *Studies in Short Fiction* 32 (Winter 1995): 75–82. The earliest and still among the most valuable treatments of Chabon's short fiction, sees the stories collected in *A Model World* as unsentimental and pessimistic, interior dramas that explore how wounded adolescents must handle memory.

Kravitz, Bennett. "The 'Aquatic Zionist' in *The Yiddish Policemen's Union*." *Studies in Popular Culture* 33.1 (2010): 96–112. Challenges critical excoriations of Chabon's novel as anti-Zionist. Explores Chabon's dark vision of the Jewish people (despite a highly entertaining plotline). Sees *The Yiddish Policemen's Union* as a dystopian historic fantasy of the failure of the Jewish people to achieve stable roots.

McCulloch, Jamie. "Creating the Rogue Hero: Literary Devices in the Picaresque Novels of Martin Amis, Richard Russo, Michael Chabon, Jonathan Safran Foer, and Steve Tesich." *International Fiction Review* 34.1–2 (2007): 13–26. Cites *Wonder Boys* as a pure example of the picaresque novel with its episodic plot, reliance on physical comedy, satire on university life, self-deprecating take on the creative process, and use of mock-heroic tone.

Meanor, Patrick. "Michael Chabon." In *American Novelists since World War II: Seventh Series*. Ed. James R. Giles and Wanda H. Giles. *Dictionary of Literary*

Biography vol. 278. Gale, 2003. www.gale.cengage.com (accessed 2 June 2013). Competent overview of Chabon's early career, centering on the themes of family, coming of age, and friendship. Includes biography.

Meyers, Helene. *Reading Michael Chabon.* Santa Barbara, Calif.: Greenwood Press, 2010. Valuable resource tool and a solid if general introduction to Chabon and his themes. Includes detailed plot summaries and character lists, compiles extensive biographical information, offers discussion questions, and includes a comprehensive bibliography of reviews.

Myers, D. G. "Michael Chabon's Imaginary Jews." *Sewanee Review* 116 (Fall 2008): 572–88. Culminating with *The Yiddish Policemen's Union,* a critique of Chabon's evolution as a Jewish writer and specifically his midcareer (re)turn to his Jewish identity. Finds Chabon's position as a Jewish American writer problematic because of characters that resist exploring the religion itself or vociferously defending the state of Israel.

Punday, Daniel. "*Kavalier & Clay:* The Comic-Book Novel and Authorship in a Corporate World." *Critique: Studies in Contemporary Fiction* 49.3 (2008): 291–303. A broad socio-economic reading of *Kavalier & Clay* that investigates how Chabon uses the experience of both Kavalier and Clay as Robinson Crusoe figures who develop and improve spiritually in the process of their work. They are able, in turn, to challenge traditional historic paradigms by empowering the individual to reshape the marketplace to an original vision rather than selling out to find success.

Shandler, Jeffrey. "Imagining Yiddishland: Language, Place, and Memory." *History and Memory: Studies in Representation of the Past* 15 (Spring-Summer 2003): 123–49. Although not centrally about Chabon, a fascinating and wide-ranging look at the context of *The Yiddish Policemen's Union* through a historic reading of the evolution of Yiddish and the creation of a homeland in post–World War II culture entirely through the vehicle of memory and language.

Singer, Marc. "Embodiments of the Real: The Counterlinguistic Turn in the Comic-Book Novel." *Critique: Studies in Contemporary Fiction* 49 (Spring 2008): 273–89. A theoretical look at *Kavalier & Clay* as part of a broad postmodern genre in which authors use comic book situations ironically to anatomize the very viability of language and to offer, in turn, a new hybrid kind of visual narrative.

Yardley, Jonathan. "The Paper Chase." Rev. of *Wonder Boys. Washington Post Book World* 19 March 1995: 3. Seminal and oft-quoted review that challenged a young Chabon to tackle broader genres and more adult themes beyond the bildungsroman.

INDEX